TOBRUK'S EASTER BATTLE 1941

The Forgotten Fifteenth's Date with Rommel's Champion

2nd Edition

John Mackenzie-Smith

First published 2014

National Library of Australia Cataloguing-in-Publication entry

Author:	Mackenzie-Smith, John H. G. (John Howard Greig), 1936-
Title:	Tobruk's Easter battle 1941 : the forgotten fifteenth's date with Rommel's champion / John Mackenzie-Smith.
Edition:	2nd edition.
ISBN:	9781925046243 (paperback)
Notes:	Previous edition: 2011.
Subjects:	Australia. Army. Battalion, 2/15th--History.
	World War, 1939-1945--Campaigns--Libya--Tobruk.
	World War, 1939-1945--Campaigns--Africa, North.
	World War, 1939-1945--Participation, Australian.
	World War, 1939-1945--Participation, German.
	Tobruk, Battles of, 1941-1942.
Dewey Number:	940.5423

Typeset in Arno Pro 12pt.

Published by Boolarong Press, Salisbury, Brisbane, Australia.

Printed and bound by Watson Ferguson & Company, Salisbury, Brisbane, Australia.

Front cover:	9th Division defending Tobruk 1941 (Australian War Memorial, Canberra)
Back cover:	4 Platoon, HQ Coy, 2/15 Bn at rest after the Tobruk siege (Russell Snow collection) with fourth and final colour patch of 2/15 Bn, 1942 (T for Tobruk)

CONTENTS

Dedicated to my mother,

Catherine "Kitty" Amelia Smith,

typifying the wives left behind by the 2/15 warriors. She gave blood throughout the conflict for the wounded, knitted in khaki for the Comforts Fund and supported prisoners-of-war from afar – while keeping the home fire burning.

PREFACE

As the seventieth anniversary of the Easter Battle at Tobruk loomed large on 14 April 2011, this volume is dedicated to the memory of those Australian, British and Indian soldiers who fought valiantly in that affray and won. It especially details the critical actions of the 2/15 Battalion whose contribution has remained unrecognised throughout that period. This arose from the long-held misconception that the Queensland battalion merely played a supporting role as a reserve unit on the perimeter while the 2/13 and 2/17 were in the thick of the action. The reality was the opposite of that misconception. The 2/15 Battalion was dug in around the Royal Horse Artillery near the distant El Adem crossroads, and was heavily involved in the final phase of the Easter Battle. Together those two units from the British Empire delivered the *coup de grace* to Lt-General Erwin Rommel's hitherto successful advance towards Tobruk.

This lack of acknowledgement led me to gently chide two of the latest Tobruk historians for their neglect of the battalion and to clear up the connected mystery of the demise of Lt-Col Gustav Ponath, Rommel's foremost infantry commander and holder of Germany's highest military decoration. While one chronicler found the tale enthralling, the other suggested I write a paper on my father, Capt Alfred Greig Smith, who, injured and unarmed, led A Company to deliver the final blow to Rommel and in the process overcame his valiant infantry opponent who chose death instead of surrender.

Thus I gradually became familiar with the major resources related to the siege of Tobruk and tried to unravel the role of the 2/15 Battalion in that battle. The intention was to write a paper for a Brisbane History Group seminar in August 2011 on the actions of Brisbane-based battalions seventy years ago. However, the project grew like 'Topsy', far exceeding the length of a half-hour presentation. Keeping an objective view of my father's role and realising the huge joint effort involved in achieving a victory, I became intrigued at what was uncovered and shared the hurt of the neglected. Accordingly a book emerged from the proposed paper.

Ironically the key to unlocking the 2/15's contribution lay in a small bundle of annotated maps, three photo albums and several critical extracts from *Caveant Hostes*, the journal of the 2/15 Battalion Remembrance Club, which my father bequeathed to me and my brother. Interviews with a few of the remaining veterans, who acknowledged my father's leadership and confirmed the battalion's location, clinched the argument. Further unearthing of the stories behind a Nazi flag and Ponath's luger, presented to my father by his company as victor on Easter Monday, added some colour to the saga. In particular, revelations arising from the stories behind those valuable resources, now residing in the Australian War Memorial (AWM), assisted in clarifying in my mind the final stages of the battle. The gallant outnumbered patrol, led by Lt Ron Yates MC, which captured a near-company strength of Ponath's crack 8 Machine-Gun Battalion, was highlighted.

The book is structured in two parts, the first being a history of the development of the 2/15 Battalion from May 1940 to the Easter Battle in April 1941 at which point I reveal the unit's baptism to battle. The second consists of supplementary articles of observations and reminiscences derived mainly from *Caveant Hostes* and a slab of Yates' correspondence. I only lightly edited those articles, preferring to let the personalities of the writers shine through. Hence their overuse of capital letters, underuse of full stops, sentences without verbs etc has escaped the red pen.

Hopefully I have shed new light on the actions of the forgotten Fifteenth. Henceforth, it is expected that the deeds of those brave Queenslanders will be recounted with pride beside those of the valiant New South Welshmen in inflicting the first defeat on Hitler's forces in World War II. Fuelled by the hurt arising from long-term neglect, some 2/15 veterans and supporters have claimed intermittently over the past seventy years that the battalion had suffered from the anti-Queensland bias of southern writers. Similar treatment by British and German authors was conveniently cast aside. This investigation has found no grounds for such flights of fantasy; there was no military or literary State-of-Origin tussle.

I wish to record my gratitude and thanks to those who have assisted me in my research and writing. The late Bob Scarr, the late Perc. Lyall, Gordon Wallace and Jack Anning, all veterans of the campaign, helped me understand the battle scene and life as a 'Rat'. Also rendering valuable assistance in checking and validating of my work were Townsville's John Neal and Steve

Rowan, secretary of the 2/15 Battalion AIF Remembrance Club. While Steve helped me out on several occasions with scanning maps which were clearer than my efforts, John proved to be a mine of information on the battalion's composition and origins. Dr William Yates unselfishly provided me with a CD of his father's valuable correspondence and Dr Mal Scarr's encouragement was heartening. Greg Snow's expertise in preparing a CD of the photos and maps to facilitate publication was typically altruistic. The videotaped interview graciously granted by Jack Anning to Steve Rowan and me was most informative and clinched my argument. Brother (Bishop) Raymond Smith's sharing of photos and memories was critical to my understanding of our father's part in the battle. Clarification of the 2/15 Bn's positions before and after the Easter Battle, was attained by an extended e-mail dialogue with my cousin Alan Smith. A former Lieutenant-Colonel, he introduced me to a variety of esoteric military records that arose from his intimate knowledge of army matters. Dr Karl James, Senior Research Officer at the AWM, read the entire manuscript and provided valuable feedback on that document and ongoing profitable communication. Chris Goddard, curator of the same institution, worked with me to ensure that the description of the Nazi flag taken near El Adem crossroads was historically valid. Further, I am honoured that the Battalion Club has supported this publication which has been a labour of love. My daughter-in-law, Christine, gallantly came to the rescue when the mysteries of technology became too much for me. Jenny and our family have, as usual, have provided unfailing encouragement and emotional support. Finally my long-time mentor and friend Dr Rod Fisher, a leading Brisbane historian, has edited and indexed this work and otherwise assisted in developing a more readable book.

John Mackenzie-Smith
5 April 2011

PREFACE TO THE SECOND EDITION

A second edition of this book has been necessary because of the importance of additional eyewitness information provided by the last surviving member of the infantry action in the King's Cross precinct which emerged after the first edition. A significant section of Chapter 5 clearly needed rewriting because the long-accepted version relating to the death of the German infantry commander proved to be incorrect. Having spent considerable time trying to evaluate the importance of the 2/15 Battalion's victory, I was determined to add this new evidence so that future researchers would have a true and unambiguous account of events.

A second edition has therefore permitted me the opportunity of tying up loose ends. I have also utilised recently unearthed 9th Australian Division analysis of the Easter Battle and the first-hand observations of B Company's crucial role in the conflict. Conscious that this volume may become the definitive version of the 2/15 battalion's involvement in the Easter Battle, I have made every effort to ensure the veracity of the testimonies given by the last survivors.

I wish to thank both Dr Barry Shaw and Dr Rod Fisher who edited and commented on the text, and the Brisbane History Group for having faith in my vision. As usual, Dan Kelly and his team at Boolarong have been helpful and proficient throughout the publication process.

John Mackenzie-Smith
Hendra
14 April 2014

INTRODUCTION

One would think that after nearly seventy years of research by both victors and vanquished about a major battle, a viable account of this important conflict would have emerged. If so, there should be little uncertainty about how events unfolded and a definitive revelation of the intrepid and brave. Unfortunately this has not been the case with the Easter Battle at Tobruk in 1941, a whole Australian battalion's involvement being unacknowledged and the associated details of a German hero's fate remaining unknown.

With the number of its veterans gravely depleted by 2005, there emerged a need to expose a new generation to this hard-fought conflict which arguably approaches the Gallipoli campaign in displays of courage, mateship and resolution. Peter Fitzsimons, an Australian journalist and popular storyteller, had the ball at his feet in 2006 and again with his attractive edition in 2009.[1] He was afforded a unique opportunity to produce a full and balanced account of the role of Australia's 20th Brigade in that legendary conflict. Along with British artillery, that untried unit inflicted the first defeat on the German juggernaut while under siege for eight months at the isolated Libyan fortress of Tobruk – commencing in Easter 1941. Further, there was a golden opportunity to venture into German literature associated with that battle. Therein might have been found the information to shed light on the mysterious demise of the brigade's unremitting antagonist, the commander of the formidable 8 Machine-Gun Bn.

By concentrating on the gallant deeds of the New South Wales battalions and providing illuminating longitudinal biographies of some of their heroes, Fitzsimons fails to acknowledge the equally gallant actions of their northern Australian comrades-in-arms. Hence authoritative pro-battalion revelations, such as provided by Barton Maughan in 1966 and repeated by Frank Harrison thirty years later, have been bypassed or ignored.[2] Some veterans of the 2/15 wrongly suspect a large dose of interstate chauvinism lies behind this neglect.

For his graphic purposes, Fitzsimons appropriately focuses on the unyielding ferocity unleashed on the Tobruk perimeter by the infantry of the other units of the 20th Brigade – the 2/13 and 2/17 Bns. Further inland, and in cohort, the batteries of the British Royal Horse Artillery bombarded the formerly invincible *Panzer*. Notwithstanding, the forgotten 2/15 Bn, the third component of the 20th Bde, was intensely involved in that conflagration, but unacknowledged. In the final analysis, it also played a vital role in countering the *blitzkrieg* that had recently cut a swathe through Poland, Belgium and France.

As Maj-Gen Leslie Morshead ordered, there was no Dunkirk-type evacuation at besieged Tobruk. Lt-Gen Erwin Rommel anticipated an easy victory, the *blitzkrieg* he launched in Europe having produced rapid, universal capitulation. It therefore came as a shock to Rommel and his *Afrika Korps* that the Australian Diggers were unyielding and put up an aggressive resistance in that god-forsaken, morale-destroying desert outpost. Consequently Robert Lyman, a graduate of Sandhurst and a highly respected military historian, who viewed the 2/15 Battalion as unworthy of mention in his account of *The longest siege,* saw cause to review that stance after wider research. He wrote: 'There is no doubt that by standing firm the 2/15 saved Tobruk from easy capture that day'.[3] However. resolution was only part of the battalion's courageous action during that battle: Maj-Gen John Lavarack, Commander of the Western Desert Force, ultimately praised the reserve battalion for its aggressive pro-activity.[4]

Ingeniously, Fitzsimons provides a clear idea of the enemy side of the conflict through research of German primary sources, such as the *8 Machine-Gun Battalion's war journal.*[5] Given that battalion's importance in defeating and pursuing the British and Australian forces in Cyrenaica up to 9 April 1941 and its central role as the vanguard of the abortive German infantry advance on Easter Monday of that year, it is appropriate that the chronicles of this brave enemy unit have been highlighted. After chasing the Allied troops in full flight from Benghazi to Tobruk, establishing the bridgehead on the perimeter of the fortress and leading the ill-fated infantry attack on Easter Sunday, that intrepid battalion was virtually wiped out. Its demise arose from the concerted efforts from all elements of the 20th Bde, the Royal Horse Artillery (RHA) and allied tanks.[6] Contrary to misconception, the 2/15 Bn played a leading role in confronting and overcoming a large group of those resolute enemy infantrymen.[7] Therein lies the source of the 2/15's first battle experience when it removed a few spokes from Rommel's unstoppable wheels.

The 'courageous and well-respected' commander of the 8 Machine-Gun Bn, a man in Rommel's mould, was 43-year-old Lt-Col Gustav Ponath. He had been plucked from preparations to invade England after playing his part in bringing about French submission. Despatched to Derna while Rommel was finishing off British resistance from the fort at Mechili, and eventually taking that coastal town with merely one battalion, Ponath cut the main highway, Via Balbia, to ambush those allies who took the inland desert route in the flight to Tobruk. This strategy was most successful in capturing 4 generals, 174 officers and 793 other ranks in the process.[8] For this and other brave feats in Germany's quest to restore Italy's honour in the Cyrenaican campaign, Ponath was awarded the Knight's Cross, Germany's highest military honour.[9] His most significant catch, Lt-Gen Sir Philip Neame VC, commander of the allied Cyrenaican forces, together with Lt-Gen Sir Richard O'Connor his adviser, was obviously a significant feat which contributed to the decision to award him that decoration.[10] He just missed snaring Morshead as another of his victims.[11]

Knighted for rolling up the Italian forces in east Libya in merely one month, O'Connor was only prevented from driving the Italians completely out of North Africa by Winston Churchill's decision to withdraw the Australian 6th Division – his most experienced unit in Libya – to help counter the German invasion of Greece.[12] The replacement for the 6th was the undertrained, untried and comparatively newly-formed 9th Australian Division, formerly the 7th Division until 26 February 1941 when the AIF was reorganised.[13] Knowing that Tobruk garrison under Italian defence had fallen in merely twenty-nine hours to the 6th, the men of the 9th, under the leadership of Morshead, were determined not to relinquish what that battle-hardened division had so valiantly gained. True to their word, the formerly untried 9th Division held out for 242 days up to the relief of the 2/13 Bn and elements of the 2/15 on 13 December 1941. Despite widespread malnutrition, exposure and attendant illness among the immovable Rats of Tobruk – a traitorous insult converted into a badge of honour – that obstruction was enshrined as the longest unconquered blockade in British and Commonwealth history. It was more remarkable in that Morshead had been instructed by Gen Archibald

Wavell, British commander in the Middle East, to hold out merely for two months to allow a British build-up in vulnerable Egypt and for the battle of El Alamein.[14]

It was well known, despite lack of detail, that Ponath was killed while leading his battalion during the last stages of the Easter Battle: Rommel's lack of reaction to his death shocked three German veterans (interviewed recently by Lyman) who were present when the news broke.[15] For nearly seventy years a mystery ensued as to the date, place and manner of his demise. Lyman maintained as late as 2009 in *The longest siege* that there was virtually no intelligence relating to the whereabouts of Ponath's death to recover his body – if only to allow closure for any surviving family and ensure that his conspicuously absent name becomes etched on the monument in Tobruk's German cemetery.[16]

For a man on the spot and writing far too early to convey the whole story in 1944, Australian war correspondent Chester Wilmot attributed Gen Heinrich von Prittwitz's death to 'Ponhardt'.[17] The battle-tried Ponath, and a foot soldier to boot, would never have directed a staff car to be driven pell-mell in the direction of the enemy – even if he knew the odds of being killed by an erratically aimed shell from one section of the eccentric 'bush artillery' were only slight.

Maughan skirted the problem. Unaware and unconcerned, the otherwise thorough writer was merely one step away from solving the puzzle.[18] The lot fell to the equally meticulous, Frank Harrison, a one-time British signaller at Tobruk, to make the connection, having read the report of a patrol written by the O/C of A Coy, 2/15 Bn and the related account of carrier action.[19] In 2009, William F Buckingham reached the same conclusion, but like Harrison, who placed the action just inside the perimeter, did not uncover the location, circumstances and details of the skirmish.[20]

Naturally the German author Wolf Heckmann consulted the *8 Machine Gun Battalion war journal* in writing *Rommel's war in Africa*. Fitzsimons subsequently obtained a translation of that document to hopefully uncover the authentic picture of the battalion's last stand from the enemy point of view.[21] By circumventing the records of the 2/15, Fitzsimons and Harrison, via Heckmann's study, attempted to determine the conditions under which Ponath died and the subsequent surrender of his troops by going 'straight to the source'. However, the guardians of the German battalion – the survivors of the Easter Battle – in their attempt to paint a more glorious demise than the actual situation, portrayed a false scenario.

As Chris Goddard of the AWM warned those who would take all war diaries at surface value: 'Contemporary accounts written by commanders ... usually contain heavy dollops of self-protection and glossing over'.[22] Apparently, the chroniclers and protectors of this German battalion's honour were no different. Ponath's illustrious record stands untouchable, beyond the romanticism created by those who set out to write their own version of history.

Thus, with a small number of exceptions, which naturally includes the battalion's chronicler,[23] it appears that, over the past seventy years, the 2/15 Bn's records, have generally been either ignored or glossed over. As late as March 2011, the AWM was still promoting the erroneous supposition that during the Easter Battle the 2/15, together with the 2/13 and 2/17, held the south-western perimeter, supported by the RHA's 25-pounders.[24] Even those who delved more deeply, failed to go further to derive the details of the Easter deployment; so that either the German version or the long-held AWM position have apparently been treated largely as gospel.

Influencing the focus of future historians, Wilmot, as the ABC war correspondent 'on the spot' in 1941, was the first of a multitude of successive authors who confined 20th Bde infantry involvement solely to the southern section of the Red Line precinct during the Easter Battle. When the Germans attacked on Good Friday, he asserted that the 2/17, alongside the 2/13 Bn, with the 2/15 in reserve, held that seventeen kilometre area astride El Adem Road.[25] Although that observation broadly applied to the long-term siege situation, it did not strictly pertain to the counter-defence arrangements during Easter 1941.

Contrary to expectations, the reserve battalion was not situated closely behind the active units on the Red line. A 20th Infantry Bde location statement issued on 10 April designated that the 2/15 Bn would act as a mobile reserve role operating from the Cegarat area (410425). From that location, it was expected to mount counterattacks in the areas controlled by the 2/17 and 2/13 when necessary.[26] However, the widely spread posts in the Cegarat precinct extended from about 4.5 kilometres north of position R 33 on the southern perimeter to 1.5 kilometres south-west of the El Adem crossroads (or King's Cross) and thereafter 4.0 kilometres north-west, mostly within the

Blue Line. Hence the impression that there was a close juxtaposition of the three battalion areas on the south-western perimeter is misleading. At any one time after Easter, two battalions from 20th Bde defended on the south-western Red Line whilst the third was rested or lay in wait well away from the action within the interior of the arena.

Significantly, the intention to deploy the 2/15 at Ceragat was promulgated on 10 April – the day on which the battalion entered the garrison, just ahead of the Germans who had pursued it eastwards along Libya's northern coastline (the Benghazi Handicap). However, unknown to Wilmot and the majority of the subsequent authors whose research was too narrowly focused, the 2/15 Bn did not take up that reserve position immediately as originally intended. On the following day, Morshead suddenly relocated this mobile reserve from the Fort Pilastrino precinct, where it was initially assigned, to a position just south-west of the El Adem crossroads – dug in around batteries of the 1 RHA (41294262).[27] The southern perimeter was held by the 2/13 and 2/17 although D and B companies of the distant and fully occupied 2/15 Bn were trucked to counterattack and offer relief in the area held by the 2/17 near the end of the ensuing battle.

A tracing dated 24 April 1941 indicates that the 2/15 Battalion did eventually occupy the Ceragat territory as the resting reserve for a short period after 21 April when the D Coy diary noted a change in location from the northern perimeter to the Blue Line or inner perimeter.[28] The battalion's war diary recorded that orders were received to take over from 2/17 on the outer perimeter on the night 23/24 April. There the battalion remained under heavy *Panzer* and artillery fire while mounting reconnaissance and fighting patrols beyond the wire until 24 May. It was then deployed back to Pilastrino (40704307) where the troops rested and swam in the Tobruk Harbour amidst sporadic shelling. By 2 June the 2/15 was again on the outer perimeter to relieve the 2/13.[29]

Given this data derived from the 2/15 Bn War Diaries, Maughan's elaborate two-page, coloured map showing dispositions on the afternoon of 5 May 1941, reproduced by Lyman in 2009, is obviously inaccurate. While the 2/15 is appropriately placed on the outer perimeter (at posts R11-R35), the 2/17 is erroneously shown as alongside – to the east – and the 2/13 is placed at rest two miles north of A Coy at the Blue Line or the inner perimeter.[30] Meanwhile the 2/10 was located in and around Fort Pilastrino.

Within the period April to June 1941 and thereafter, the 2/15 Bn did indeed hold the southern boundary either with the 2/13 or the 2/17 as asserted by Wilmot. However, this was not the situation that existed during the Easter Battle which preceded that phase. During combat the 2/15 Bn, far from the Red Line on the southern frontier, was vigorously defending the location in the north which Rommel deemed to be the most important point in Tobruk's defences. This was never acknowledged in Wilmot's writing. He seems to have considered that the 2/15 eagerly waited at the ready in the wings while the infantry of 2/13 and 2/17 took care of most of the infantry action. Accordingly, Wilmot's successors erroneously limited the intense infantry counteraction on Easter Monday merely to that area just north of the Red Line, no action being cited within the planned Blue Line sector.

Wilmot provided a most informative map of the Easter Battle in his book on *Tobruk 1941*, showing the RHA's postion just below the El Adem crossroads and the sudden U-turn taken by the *Panzers* in their swift advance and retreat. However, it is an enigma that he later denied there had been a tank battle in the vicinity.[31] It is especially puzzling to reconcile that denial with his statement that the *Panzers* came within 600 metres of the RHA's 25-pounders which were dug in one mile south-west of the crossroads.[32] BH Liddell-Hart, editor of *The Rommel papers* asked Wilmot to comment on Rommel's claim, which arose when he finally took Tobruk in 1942, that the presence of several wrecked tanks in the vicinity of the crossroads 'showed that they had reached the hill and thus gained the most important point of the Tobruk defences'. Astonishingly he inferred Rommel was incorrect: the *Panzer* wrecks had been towed to their positions as target practice for British anti-tank guns![33]

As Wilmot has always been regarded as an authority, subsequent chroniclers of the Easter Battle, with the exception of Barton Maughan – who located the 2/15 by inference – have followed a false trail. They were literally in the thick of that RHA-*Panzer* battle.[34] Thus the southern battalions have deservedly earned accolades for over seven decades, while their northern comrades at arms have been unjustly accorded the serial disregard which Wilmot implied was their lot. In the final count, his uneven knowledge of the Australian deployment on Easter Monday 1941, delivered with an air of readily accepted authority, appears to be related to the 2/15 Bn's neglect in Australian, British and German military history. When all was said and done, the battalion that Wilmot lost during the Easter Battle thereafter became forgotten.

Yet there was hope when Harrison in 1999 and Buckingham in 2009, demonstrating more flexible thinking than their colleagues, discarded the Wilmot straightjacket and broadened their research bases to include the 2/15 Bn's war diary. Not going far enough to determine its battle location, they discovered two independently written but synchronised reports of a 2/15 raid on Easter Monday 1941. One was by a sergeant commanding two Bren Gun carriers and the other by a seemingly anonymous OC of A Coy of that battalion.[35] Therein rest the unblemished and unevaluated facts as unearthed by Maughan: just enough for Buckingham to broadly solve the Ponath riddle.

Proceeding one step further, future investigators have the opportunity to derive the critical details from grass-roots primary sources, both oral and written – the former becoming more urgent as the years pass by. Such research should focus on interviews of veterans for their recollections along with personal reminiscences and first-hand accounts published in the battalion's Remembrance Club's journals. This kind of basic resource is ignored by too many writers. Consequently hitherto unreported incidents of the battalion's valour will radically change the long-held misconception that the 2/15 contributed little of significance to the Easter Battle.

PART I:

A HISTORY OF THE 2/15 BATTALION TO EASTER 1941

chapter 1

FROM BRISBANE TO THE FRONT LINE

In 1995 Ron Austin provided a detailed account of the genesis of the 2/15 Bn in his comprehensive book *Let Enemies Beware*. Having scoured the appropriate war diaries and veterans' reminiscences, he presented an authentic account of the battalion's fortunes – from Brisbane to Borneo via Tobruk.[36] The genesis of the battalion is particularly well covered.

Following the dispatch of the 6th Div to the Middle East in January 1940, the Australian War Cabinet decided to form the 7th Div. Comprising the 19th, 20th and 21st Bdes, the proposed 7th was placed under the command of Maj-Gen John Lavarack from 4 April. Brig John Murray assumed the rank of CO of the 20th Brigade. Consisting of the 2/13 and 2/17 Bns, recruited in New South Wales and the 2/15 Bn derived from Queensland sources, that brigade was destined to win battle laurels initially in Africa. Accordingly, when Lt-Col Robert Marlan, a World War I veteran and Brigade Major, was appointed CO of the battalion from 26 April 1940, he swiftly undertook the critical task of selecting his officers by visiting militia units operating throughout Queensland.

From 1 May, Maj Charles Barton, knighted as Queensland's Co-ordinator General in the post-war period, was appointed 2/IC. Capt Andrew Skinner DCM MM, a member of the original 15th Bn and career officer, was selected as Quarter Master. Among the battalion's first commissioned officers were Lts Bill Williams, Greig Smith of the 61st Battalion (Cameron Highlanders) and future Military Cross winners FL (Lance) Bode, WW (Bill) Cobb and RA (Ron) Yates – all from Hughenden district's 26th Bn. Recent Duntroon graduate, Lt AL MacDonald, future Chief of the Defence Forces and the battalion's other knight, was assigned to HQ.

John Neal, son of Ernest John (Bomber) Neal OBE, one time RSM of the battalion, explains how the unit was formed:

> ... it was basically drawn from elements of 11th Bde which was in camp at Miowera. The brigade was made up of 26th Bn (Longreach, Hughenden and Cloncurry); 31st Bn (Townsville region); 42nd Bn (Capricornia region) and 51st Bn (Cairns region.) The

> way the battalion was set up was that the CO tended to keep old CMF members in the same Coy in the Bn, for example 26th Bn members went into A Coy, 31st Bn went into B Coy etc. 26th Bn was merged with 15th Bn known for administrative purposes as the Oxley Rgt. In this manner there tended to be camaraderie within each Coy.[37]

By 25 May an adequate number other ranks had been recruited to mount a rather untidy battalion parade – top heavy in officers at that stage – at the HQ which had recently been relocated to Redbank near Ipswich. An understanding Brig Murray took the salute. However, when the battalion band was formed, containing a core from the Gympie City Band, its salutary effect on the battalion's bearing and marching was plainly evident.[38] Regardless, 'Spike' Marlan, never let up, fully realising that among his troops was a large component from the west – a rough and ready lot of station hands, ringers, stockriders and others with bush and firearm skills. To his credit, and that of his officers and NCOs, he eventually shaped them into a fine, battalion-proud, warrior force.

The CO certainly expected high standards from himself, his officers and his troops. Immediately he set out to mould a cohesive and efficient unit from the disorganised intake which hailed from widely dissimilar backgrounds and possessed disparate attitudes, behaviours and skills. He aimed to instil smartness, pride and alertness through battalion parades; strengthen endurance by long route marches; and promote fitness by a wide range of sports. So dedicated was Marlan to achieve his objective that he nearly asphyxiated his battalion which was required at the end of one parade to complete the march-off phase wearing gas masks.

From the beginning of June, recruits without prior military training were given intensive instruction by five experienced AIC instructors and the ubiquitous, bellowing NCOs from within the battalion. Thereafter, under the keen eye of RSM Cec Guest, the battalion was able to partake of a common syllabus centred on precision drill – foot, rifle and bayonet. Shooting live rounds at the Enoggera Rifle Range quickly followed. Gradually the intensive training was reaping results, and a fit, highly integrated unit was emerging: fully outfitted, smart in appearance, competently trained, precise in drill and battalion proud.[39]

GARRISON DUTY AT DARWIN

On 1 July 1940, the battalion, recently vaccinated and decked out in newly issued tropical garb, set sail aboard the SS *Zealandia* for garrison duty at Darwin. It was in that northern outpost where cohesion was finally secured and camaraderie forged. For a start, the group effort to make their quarters liveable at the long-neglected Vestey Meatworks gave the men pride in their surroundings and appreciation of good hygiene while fostering cooperation. A series of battalion parades, frequent inter-company sporting competitions, stints at road construction and the hard labour required to set up Darwin's defences contributed significantly to fitness, strength and stamina. Long marches to mount the guard at Knuckey's Lagoon naval base, digging defence trenches and regular stoushes with members of the crack Mobile Defence Force in Darwin's main streets also unified and toughened the battalion. Concert parties, Chinese gambling dens and pubs provided the bulk of its entertainment.[40]

Perhaps one of the most important innovations, one which would have a profound effect on the subsequent performance of the battalion on the front line, was the formation of the Carrier platoon within Head Quarters Coy. Under the command of Lt MacDonald, its 42 members were trained systematically to fire the Vickers Machine Gun and manoeuvre the carriers powered by v8 motors which produced speeds of up to 40mph. Membership of this platoon provided a welcome relief to those who considered the life of an infantryman in the tropics to be deadly dull. Later members of this new platoon were rostered to perform highly responsible anti-aircraft guard duties on the troopship carrying them overseas.[41]

Don Parker recalled that the move back to Brisbane was undertaken in two parts. A, B and part of C Coys comprised the first party of 370 personnel which moved out on 27 September 1940. Once again they sailed on the SS *Zealandia*. During that ship's return voyage to Darwin she transported the 2/25th Bn, thereby enabling the remainder of the 2/15 to travel southwards to Brisbane on 23 October. It was not until 7 November that they were able to join the advance party at their Redbank base.

Three days later the battalion was sent on pre-embarkation leave: the destination was unknown. All returned to base in time to be 'hardened up' by a long (18 mile) moonlight route march with full packs, firing live .303 rifle ammunition on the range and having numerous bayonet practices. At the last minute a long-overdue introduction to the Bren Light Machine Gun (the look and listen but don't touch type of instruction) was given by a young officer.[42] Finally, the battalion's stay at Redbank Camp concluded with an Open Day, a unit parade and an address by Lt-Col Marlan. Brisbane also had a chance to bid the battalion an enthusiastic farewell at a well-attended parade through the city. Previously Brig Murray and the Prime Minister Robert Gordon Menzies, probably knowing the unit's secret destination, visited the camp.

George Alford recollected that after several false starts due to the presence of a German raider around the north-west coast of Australia, the battalion received orders to move out on 25 December 1940. Wearing heavy winter uniforms and toting packs weighing nearly 100lbs in the middle of a hot summer, the troops were near exhaustion after the long march to Redbank railway station where they were to entrain for South Brisbane Interstate Railway Station. Destined for Sydney, the battalion members, wearing a new colour patch – the second of four – were warmly farewelled by a large, enthusiastic crowd of relatives and friends.

VOYAGE TO SUEZ AND ONTO GAZA

On Boxing Day 1940, troops of the 2/15 Bn detrained at Darling Harbour prior to a swift ferry trip to HT *Queen Mary* (officially QX), the second largest ship afloat. Nearby, similar converted liners, forming the remainder of convoy – HTs *Aquitania* (the flagship), *Mauretania, Awatea* and *Dominion Monarch* – were taking aboard their allocations of military passengers. Over 6000 personnel crammed into *QX*, many of the other ranks having to sleep and eat in shifts.

After departure on 28 December, the troops had every reason to feel secure, being protected by such a swift, well-armed escort vessel as the cruiser HMAS *Canberra* and reassured by the superior speed of QX. On one occasion, north of Fremantle, following a reliable warning that a German warship was in the vicinity, *QX* demonstrated it had more up its sleeve to counteract threats from enemy submarines, not only by weaving and frequent changes in course but also by its incredibly fast speed. On that occasion, the former Cunard liner unbelievably reached a speed of 29 knots, its stern settling down near the waterline and its bow pointing skywards.[43]

Meanwhile training continued on the main deck and the companies entered teams in the ship's sports meeting. The Equator was crossed with appropriate ceremony by Father Neptune and the band provided several concerts on the quarter deck. Companies were allocated permanent duties, D Coy being required, for instance, to mount a permanent picket on both sides of the promenade deck. Time was hardly wasted; lectures by officers, anti-gas measures, first aid and map reading kept the men occupied. On the recreational side, the sedate card tournaments, such as the padre's euchre party, were offset by vigorous physical tussles such as tug-o-war and boxing tournaments. Both of the latter were dominated by rough and tough A Coy platoon from which commander Lt Bode emerged as one of the battalion's best pugilists. Capt Ted Peek, OC of D Coy, recorded that HQ Coy was defeated in merely 'two straight pulls – [A Coy being] the first rifle Coy to manage this feat.'[44]

After standing outside Fremantle harbour until 4 January 1941, the convoy traversed the Indian Ocean, lying anchor at Trincomalee in northern Ceylon [Sri Lanka] a week later. On 14 January, the battalion transferred to the uncomfortably cramped, sparsely victualled and decidedly grubby Dutch ship, HT300 *Indrapoera*. In that ship, the troops had their first surprise-filled encounters with the commonplace European bidets or *sanitaires douches*, conveniences unknown to insular Australians at that time. After a day's shore leave at Colombo, the battalion joined a flotilla which had grown to 13 troop ships (eventually 15), all under the protection of the cruiser HMAS *Anterior* and light cruiser HMS *Capetown*. Despite initial disappointment with the ship, the vessel was exclusively the domain of the 2/15 Bn, creating a cohesive body of troops and unit pride. The common destination for this unified military group, forged by its determined CO and shaped by the intimate confines, was the Suez Canal via the Red Sea – the gateway to Egypt, Palestine and Libya.

The troops had every opportunity to become up-to-date with current affairs while ship-bound: the British drive to expel the Italians from Cyrenaica was naturally given prominence in the early, regular on-board news sheets. The professionally published *Ships Flashes* on *QX* and the unpretentious *Indrapoera News* produced by the Dutch ship were circulated daily to that end. While passengers learned details of the fall of Bardia and the thrust towards Tobruk in the former publication, they read about the ultimate fall of that Italian garrison to the Australian 6th Div AIF via the latter medium.[45] Hence

D Coy's war diary recorded that the rumour which had circulated the ship on 22 January regarding Tobruk's capitulation was confirmed on the following day via maritime telegraph. Capt Peek wrote: 'It was officially announced in the "Indrapoera News" bulletin today, that Tobruk had fallen to the AIF after a wonderful charge through gaps in their outer defences'.[46] Consequently on Sunday 26 January, Chaplain CSC Arkell conducted special shipboard services to commemorate Australia Day with thanksgiving for the victories of the AIF in Libya.

When the convoy entered the Gulf of Suez early in the afternoon of Monday 27 January, the formation of the ships was changed to single file: the *Indrapoera* lay eleventh in line. Two days later, after steaming ahead very slowly, the convoy eventually entered the Suez Canal. The ships were then detained for a further three days in the Great Bitter Lake while Wellington bombers from the RAF, fitted with circular magnetic mine detonation devices on their undercarriages, cleared the area of explosive devices. These had recently been dropped by enemy aircraft after a nocturnal raid on a nearby British base. Regardless, the ship's lifeboats were lowered to provide the men with much-needed exercise. Coinciding with news that Derna had fallen to the British, the convoy resumed its voyage up the canal on Sunday 3 February.

In the extra time made available by the above interruption to progress, the battalion packed ready for disembarkation, kit bags were issued and rifles checked. The troops were also made familiar with customs and practices inherent in Palestine's Arab/Moslem civilisation, each soldier being provided with a pamphlet entitled 'What of Palestine? Pointers for the AIF'. While the troops were directed to be respectful and quiet in mosques and to be aware that the Arabs' standard of honesty differed from that of most Australians, they were counselled to take no corrective action when they encountered males riding on donkeys while women walked behind carrying the heavy loads. The leaflet advised: 'Do not attempt to teach the Arab Australian customs. His wife is used to this, do not interfere'.[47]

GAZA

On 3 February 1941 the battalion was able to enter the canal, the ship arriving at El Kantara where they good-naturedly entrained in cattle trucks bound for Kilo 89, a training camp on Gaza Ridge. There they joined the 2/13 and 2/17

Bns thereby completing the 20th Bde under training in Palestine. Cpl Alex Connor remembered Kilo 89 as 'a tented encampment alongside a bitumen road with a citrus orchard to the north of the Bn lines. Sand everywhere and no trees or vegetation'.[48]

There the battalion formed close links with members of the other 'sister' units, especially the 2/13. It was toughened up by reluctantly adapting to daylight saving, enduring long route marches across the strength-sapping sandy desert, digging tank traps and drains, filling in old trenches and improving existing air-raid facilities. Football training and playing in the battalion Rugby Union competition became the most popular aspects of building physical and mental strength. The ensuing match against the 2/13 team was won by the 2/15 which was able to field a former Wallaby, not to mention a formidable forward pack drawn from A Coy's invincible tug o' war squad. Concurrently, the Gaza Police soccer team was soundly beaten by the battalion XI.

After taking the salute at the first battalion parade on 5 February, Brig Murray complimented the battalion which performed creditably after so long at sea. Capt Peek was chuffed that the CO refrained from criticising a subsequent parade while the men considered it an honour and proof they had not lost the high standard achieved at Darwin. As for weapon training, systematic introduction to and firing of the Bren Light Machine-Gun were undertaken successfully. Under instruction from members of the 'sister' battalions, all members fired the gun in both automatic and single shot modes on the Jaffa Range. Tank hunting, bayonet practice and night patrols, along with preparation of platoon and Coy defences, completed the battalion's training for strenuous desert warfare ahead.[49] Still, the brigade, with merely two light machine guns at its disposal, was seriously lacking in weapons and equipment.

Causing much heartache, some of the battalion were left behind when the Brigade ultimately struck camp to form the Australian Infantry Training Bn. Established at Murghazi outside Gaza, that new battalion formed a training unit for reinforcements and those returning to their units after hospitalisation.[50]

CROSSING CYRENAICA TO THE FRONT LINE

At 0130hrs on Friday 28 February 1941, following a march to Gaza station and crossing the Suez in punts, the battalion entrained en route to West Kantara station. This time they travelled in comfortable carriages instead of stock wagons. The ultimate destination was still unknown at that juncture. Traversing the fertile Nile delta and travelling well north of Cairo, the battalion moved to Mersa Matruh on 1 March. There they were trucked for two miles to 'abandoned, bombed, concrete sleeping quarters – no doors or windows' – a former outpost of the Egyptian army. [51]

On the rail journey to Mersa Matruh, the troops were able for the first time to see practical examples of defensive works. The Egyptians had formed those for protection against an expected Italian offensive prior to Gen O'Connor's wrap-up. Capt Peek observed: 'Tank traps such as we had read about but never seen extended to the horizon on either side of the line, miles of barbed wire in double aprons ... and plenty of 'asparagus beds' of both steel rail and concrete were in evidence'.[52] Mersa Matruh itself featured perimeter defences of minefields and barbed wire.

As the CO informed the battalion at the parade on 2 March, prior to yet another route march in the sand, they were henceforth on active duty. The men learned that they were to cross the Libyan Desert in a long convoy with other troops of the 20th Bde to relieve the forward posts of the 6th Div and guard the post of Mersa Brega – the limit of the British advance. At 0745hrs on 3 March the convoy led by Brigade HQ undertook active service, getting used to the sight of abandoned equipment including vehicles, field guns, tanks, rifles and even planes. These had been strewn by retreating Italian troops or destroyed in battle on either side of the road. Ultimately 'the sight of pieces of flotsam left by war failed to interest them because of its monotonous regularity'.[53] Unfortunately the not so obvious land mines and booby traps left behind by the Italians claimed two soldiers from the 2/13 on 3 March at Bug Bug (or Buq Buq) near a deserted hospital. On a brighter note the battalion later demonstrated a sustained interest in acquiring samples of the copious quantities of abandoned Italian wine, tinned food and cigarettes. Further, they quickly saw the irony of being conveyed in Italian lorries by 6th Div drivers. Connor recalled: 'The sight of all the troops in one great convoy moving ahead and behind in one snaking line was a magnificent sight'.[54]

The convoy left rough roads and Egypt behind on 4 March, travelling on Mussolini's excellent Via Balbia to Tobruk by way of Bardia which was protected by a wide tank trap and an intricate barbed-wire fence. Nearby Tobruk possessed the only good harbour between Alexandria and Benghazi, not to mention its invaluable water plant and natural springs. It was there they were introduced to Italian weapons and the *khamsin* – a fierce storm of whirling fine sand which clogged up every opening, clung to every surface and reduced visibility to a matter of feet. Wearing goggles was necessary to avoid blindness and movement was virtually impossible until the wind storm abated. By digging deep trenches three miles outside the western perimeter of that garrison, the men managed to protect themselves from the swirling, freezing eddy for two nights and slept soundly.

On the road to Tocra on 6 March the convoy was attacked by Heinkel dive bombers, killing an officer and wounding a soldier from 2/13 Bn. On passing through Derna, a British ammunition truck was riddled with bullets as was the leg of the WO who was riding in it. Accordingly, special precautions were taken to deal with harassment from enemy aircraft by placing an AA sentry at the rear of each vehicle. Despite imminent danger, Capt Peek was able to admire the magnificent view of the white-washed town of Derna from the steep road winding down through a mountain pass down. Appreciating the quality of Italian workmanship in building that highway, he considered it to be 'a lasting monument to the surveyors, engineers and road workers who designed and built it'.[55] When the convoy bypassed the beautiful city of Benghazi on 8 March, following an evening bivouac at Tocra, its avenue of eucalypts would have evoked the nostalgic admiration of all Australians.

Nevertheless the troops were brought back to earth with the knowledge that they were approaching the front line. It lay thirty miles south of Agedabia where the battalion bedded down on the night of 8 March Earlier the 2/13 had detached from the convoy at Beda Fomm. After reaching Agedabia, the 2/15 continued its run of good luck as all members managed to refill their canteens moments before the water point was bombed. Regrettably the following British units missed out on access to the water and suffered twelve casualties in the assault.

That night, advance parties left to take up positions on the front line at Kilo 789 near Mersa Brega. The main body of the 2/15 Bn followed two days later to relieve elements of the 2/5 and 2/7 Bns of the 6th Bde, thereby becoming the most advanced troops in the British lines. While B, C and D Coys occupied the marshes on the left flank and the village, A Coy as the reserve took up positions on Cemetery Hill on 11 March. It was located forward of the general line of defence. The 2/17 Bn guarded the rear of the battalion.[56] Austin estimated that they were located half a mile east of the village, astride of the main route to Agedabia.

While occupying this extreme position, the battalion was in dire straits. It severely lacked the basic materiel needed to defend against the well equipped enemy's might:

> ... the Carrier platoon had reverted to an infantry role. There was no equipment. No carriers, no Brens, no anti tank rifles or guns, no radio, no telephone. Some of the men had .303 rifles built in 1908. The Bn had no motor transport. There was virtually no aircraft protection for a hundred miles. One Bofor gun was available for the Brigade. The HQ Coy had little to do except carry out patrols.[57]

The battalion remained at Mersa Brega until 22 March. Apart from the unfortunate mine-related death of Pte Kelvin Croker from B Coy while on patrol and the Luftwaffe's ineffective daily bombing, life in the vicinity of that settlement was relatively uneventful. Patrols to all points of the compass, one being Lt Arthur MacDonald's forty-five mile reconnaissance mission towards El Agheila with two armoured cars, revealed signs of enemy tanks and vehicles. On another patrol, Lt Bode's group from A Coy moved so close to the enemy as to hear them speaking.

chapter 2

BENGHAZI HANDICAP AND THE PONATH FACTOR

The presence of German armour and build-up of troops in the forward area were only too apparent.[58] Signs, which indicated that an advance by Rommel and his *Afrika Korps* was imminent, prompted the Allied Command to order a withdrawal to Egypt. There it was expected that Allied troops would gather for a decisive show-down with the Nazi *blitzkrieg* machine. That strategic retreat, incorporating the decision to abandon ruined Benghazi and to temporarily defend Tobruk, with its vital harbour, became known as the Benghazi Handicap or the Tobruk Derby.

Initially, Gen O'Connor ordered the 9th Div to withdraw to Derna (and later to El Gazala). Hoping that Rommel would discontinue his pursuit after taking Benghazi, the British 3rd Armoured Div made its way across the desert to the Mechili garrison. To cover this mass retirement the 20th Bde AIF was required to hold Er Regima.[59]

Casting the textbook aside, Rommel decided to keep on the heels of the British, dividing his forces into three and driving them forward relentlessly – even dropping instructions from his self-piloted *Fiedler Storch* aircraft and landing beside units if he considered their progress to be excessively tardy. The 3rd Reconnaissance Bn and elements of the Italian 27th Brescia Div under Maj-Gen Heinrich Kirchheim were sent north and east along the excellent coastal road, pursuing the British forces which took that route leading to Benghazi and beyond. In the centre a force consisting principally of Maj-Gen Johannes Streich's 5th *Panzer* Rgt and elements of the Italian 132nd *Ariete* (Italian armoured division) drove across the desert to the common destination – the fortress of Mechili. Located at the junction of a network of caravan routes, the British had gathered in force at that ancient stronghold. On the far right were sited a battalion from *Ariete* and elements of Streich's 5th Light Motorised Div. Subsequently at Mechili, Rommel eliminated half of Cyrenaica's command in one fell stroke and thereby controlled half of that province. To complete the reconquest of Cyrenaica, all he had to do was to deal with the other half – the 9th Australian Div which he regarded as not only badly trained and ill-equipped, but a certain 'push-over'.[60]

THE TOBRUK DERBY AND PONATH'S APPEARANCE

The precursor to that ignominious retreat originated when Rommel's 5th Light Bn took El Agheila on 24 March 1941 – two days after the badly equipped 2/15 was directed to withdraw from Mersa Brega. That unit took up positions near El Abiar, a nine-mile march from Er Regima which overlooked Benghazi then under strategic demolition; even the sewerage system was destroyed. Neither the fall of El Agheila nor the subsequent rout at Mersa Brega on 31 March was known to the 2/15 Bn because of intra-brigade communication deficiencies.[61] On 4 April, under orders from Gen O'Connor, the 9th Div was directed to hold Er Regima until forced to withdraw.[62]

Following O'Connor's orders, the 2/15 Bn was transported through Barce, taking up defensive positions on top of an escarpment overlooking the town to mount rear guard action. The 20th Bde was told to defend the escarpment east of Benghazi, especially the road and railway at the Er Regima Pass. On 27 March that task fell to the 2/13 Bn while the 2/15 dug defensive positions eight miles away near El Abair to patrol the railway towards Benghazi. While A Coy was left to defend the road, D Coy became the forward unit and did not stop firing until it left Barce. In the one instance of action against a German convoy, the leading vehicle was taken out with a Breda while rifle and Bren fire 'collected the lot'.[63]

After Benghazi was 'liberated' by the enemy on 3 April, the immovable 2/13 was again attacked at Barce. The German force consisting of 16 tanks, armoured cars and 2000 infantry inflicted significant casualties on the Australians, amounting to 82 killed and 16 wounded.

When the Germans encircled Mechili with a brilliant flanking movement on 8 April they took 2000 prisoners, including Maj-Gen Michael Gambier-Perry. It was only the courageous last stand by the Indian Motor Bde which enabled most of the British forces in Cyrenaica to escape to fight another day. 'Two Australian brigades as well as the bulk of the anti-tank and artillery units had managed to extricate themselves ....'[64] Accordingly, Morshead demanded a swift, orderly withdrawal to El Gazala via Derna so that the 9th Div would not be cut off.[65] For his part, Rommel ordered Maj-Gen Streich to head east for the coast without delay, the ultimate aim being to capture the fleeing brigade and take Tobruk. He boasted that the Suez Canal would be taken in the summer.

Capt Peek recorded on 7 April that beautiful Derna was mostly aflame, the streets being congested with traffic right up to the pass. Connor was intrigued with the scene that lay before him as he awoke in a truck en route to Tobruk from Derna:

> We could see stretched out before us a huge dusty undulating plain. No grass, no trees, no habitation, simply a mass of dust covered transport of all makes and purposes, fleeing steadily eastward to Tobruk. The vehicles were constantly changing direction to circumvent natural obstacles and no unit formation existed.[66]

Nevertheless they managed to arrive unscathed in the midst of a dust storm at El Gazala and later at Acroma which had been in German hands on the previous evening.

Major John Devine, an Australian medical officer who tended the sick and wounded in the British Casualty Clearing Station at Derna, was also involved in that retreat to Tobruk. He had derived extreme pleasure working in that 'small green oasis at the foot of the hills' between the bright blue Mediterranean and 'the torn and wadi-riven stony desert'. Joining the withdrawal in an Italian diesel truck without lights, he recalled the nightmare of a journey as the convoy negotiated numerous hairpin bends to ascend the 1500 feet precipitous escarpment. The roadsides were littered with overturned, abandoned and burning vehicles. His convoy was apparently very lucky to get through as a number of preceding trucks had been captured and set on fire by an enemy patrol of armoured cars.[67]

Devine was obviously referring to that situation which resulted in the decapitation of the headquarters from the 2/15 Bn on 7 April at Derna, leaving only a body of four rifle companies. Connor left little doubt as to the captor's identity when the large group of Australians joined the British prisoners taken the previous day:

> Captured with the group were General O'Connor, and two other very senior British leaders. Eventually the mass of men were instructed to get up, form threes and prepare to march to Derna. The group, being a mixture and lacking the usual leadership of their own NCO's was lethargic. In no time the German colonel, a most dynamic man armed with a sub machine gun, swung into action and left no doubt in

> any man's mind that he expected us to be ready in about one minute or else he would shoot. This proved to be a most effective solution. This particular colonel became well known for his drive, courage and personality. Everyone who became a prisoner even later had some knowledge of the man and all conceded he was a top class man. ... Even his own men ran when he spoke and his motor cyclists and drivers never ceased to move their equipment at top speed.[68]

This was the battalion's introduction to Lt-Col Gustav Ponath, commander of the 8 Machine-Gun Bn. One of Rommel's right-hand men, Ponath's achievements in Cyrenaica were about to be acknowledged with Germany's highest military decoration. Mostly in the vanguard of Rommel's version of *blitzkrieg,* he similarly eschewed inflexible planning, struck with speed and took advantage of beneficial situations as they presented themselves. Further, his unpredictability often caught his foes on the wrong foot thereby making him a master of surprise. By such speed and guile he had deprived the 2/15 Bn of their CO, their 2/IC and over 150 comrades-at-arms on a back track outside Derna.

Born in 1898, Ponath saw action in Poland in 1939 as major and commander of the 50th Infantry Div. He was subsequently promoted to Lt-Colonel and an instructor of infantry tactics at Dresden. Ultimately he assumed command of the 8 Machine-Gun Bn in July 1940, serving in Brittany. After Hitler abandoned plans to invade the United Kingdom, Ponath's battalion was detached from Operation Sea Lion and assigned to Streich's 5th Light Motorised Div (5LMD). He was thenceforth an integral part of principal striking force in Rommel's *Afrika Korps.*

Alongside other soldiers of the incomplete *Korps,* Ponath's men rode astride their distinctive BMW motorcycles with side-car occupants toting Mauser MG 34s [machine guns]. Ostentatiously they paraded through Tripoli during Rommel's triumphant entry on 15 February 1941.[69] From that moment, he brushed aside the Army High Command's (OKH) order to implement a holding operation against the British and delay offensive action in Cyrenaica until May when the 15th *Panzer* Div was expected to arrive. While Rommel contemptuously deflected similar directives from his nominal Italian superior, Gen Italo Gariboldi, he saw a golden opportunity to free Cyrenaica for the Italians and swiftly conquer Northern Egypt with its Suez Canal prize. Even with his limited forces, he felt sure he could defeat the British before they built up their defences. In turn, having cracked the German Enigma code, the British were lulled into a sense of false security, assuming that Rommel would follow Hitler's directive to delay his assault. 'For him everything depended on swift reaction to unforeseeable contingencies that threw the best-laid plans awry'.[70]

As events unfolded, Ponath was allocated a prominent part to play in achieving that plan in attacking north of the coast road. After a prolonged period of air and ground reconnaissance, El Agheila fell to Lt-Col Herbert Olbrich's 5th *Panzer* Rgt and Streich's 5th Light Div on 24 March without opposition. Similarly the defence of Mersa Brega collapsed seven days afterwards. At a speed which amazed Rommel after Agedabia, the capital of Cyrenaica was abandoned on 2 April and the British strategically withdrew northward and eastward in columns of vehicles in front of the German advance. Much to Churchill's chagrin, Lt-Gen Neame decided not to defend the tactically demolished Benghazi which fell on 3 April.

At Agedabia, Maj-Gen Gambier-Parry's 2nd Armoured Div beat back the initial attack of the 5th Light Div. It was Ponath's action which turned the tide of the battle. His well-trained infantry was sent into the British flank, forcing its commander to cleverly withdraw. Heckmann, the German author, commented: 'Making skilful use of cover provided by the dunes, [the 8 Machine-Gun Bn] made obsolete the old-fashioned British book of rules which was based on the assumption of an orderly battlefield with neatly separated lines on which one had especially to be wary of being outflanked or encircled'.[71]

However, this conflict demonstrated that British cruiser tanks with 2-pounder guns and the RHA's 25-pounders were more than a match for the *Panzer* Mark III. Furthermore the latter would cause significant damage to the new, heavily armoured *Panzer* Mark IV – over open sights – when it saw action.

On 6 April, Morshead discovered that Rommel was only 48 miles south of Derna while most of his division was located 100 miles to the west of that location. Hence the Australians faced the prospect of being cut off by the German advance. Deciding not to stand firm at Barce and knowing that Benghazi was to be abandoned, the Australians spent the next four days making their way via the clogged coast road, with two newly acquired carriers, first to Derna and then El Gazala.[72] Although the retreat had been going on since 24 March, this was the phase generally known as the Benghazi Handicap.

Jack Anning recalled that the 2/15 Bn did not have its own transport, progressing in a leap-frog manner towards its destination. Transports of a particular battalion would deposit their consignees at their destination and then double back to pick up the 2/15. Piecemeal, step-by-step, they made their way to Tobruk.[73]

THE 9TH DIVISION MALIGNED

Gen Neame wrote a scathing letter on 30 March 1941 to Gen Morshead regarding discipline and control within the 9th Div, citing incidents of drunkenness, theft, disobedience, stealing, shooting, pilfering supplies and rustling which had occurred on a large scale ever since the Australians arrived at Barce. Expressing his contempt for such soldiers who lacked discipline, sobriety and obedience to orders, Neame closed Benghazi and Barce to most of the troops and requested Morshead to do all in his power to enforce military law and expectation. Focusing on the Australian officers, he blamed them for the apparent lawlessness as they 'seldom do enforce discipline or orders and more often endeavour to condone or whitewash the offence'. He considered that they were incapable of commanding their men and concluded: 'Your Division will never be a useful instrument of war unless and until you can enforce discipline.' In fact Neame argued, such men who behaved in this manner were helping the enemy.[74]

Although Morshead took immediate remedial action, it is a matter for conjecture to attribute Neame's loss of his command on 3 April to the reactions to that letter which were forwarded by Morshead to Gen Thomas Blamey and Field Marshall Archibald Wavell, General Officer Commanding the 2 AIF and Commander in Chief of the Middle East respectively. Both were fully conversant with the irreverent style of the valiant Australian troops in World War I. Moreover there was a suspicion abroad that Neame was transferring his poor relationship with the all-conquering 6th Div to the untried 9th.

Rommel also harboured prejudice towards the Australians, considering them to be badly trained, inexperienced and a poorly armed rabble. Yet he saw cause to eat his words after encountering the much maligned 9th Div in battle. He noted that the Australians fought with remarkable tenacity; even the wounded stayed in the fight until their last breath. Moreover he was impressed with the bearing and style of those 60 prisoners paraded before him: 'immensely big and powerful men, who without question represented an elite formation of the British Empire, a fact that was evident in battle'.[75]

Likewise Ponath had to reconsider his negative attitude towards the 9th Div before the month was out. The 8 Machine-Gun Bn was originally part of Streich's group, but outdistanced the parent unit by 5 April. He was sent to Mechili on the following day and then north to cut the coast road in both directions at Derna on the 7th with merely one company of his battalion and later with elements of the 5th *Panzer* Rgt. Having travelled 450 miles through mostly trackless desert, his mission was to 'regain the coastal road ... and deny it to the retreating British units'.[76]

Exhausted, thirsty and sleep-deprived, Ponath's group moved slowly but relentlessly north-west across 'the Cyrenaican bulge'. They moved along a track described by locals as 'suicidal' and 'appalling.' Rommel had personally conducted them to Derna during the night, not pausing for time-wasting sleep. Despite that, the relatively small group, later supported by combat troops led by Generals Schwerin and Olbrich, had taken 800 prisoners on the way. After a detachment of Ponath's motorcycle troops captured Generals Neame and O'Connor,[77] his forces knocked out the last four operational tanks of the 5th Royal Tank Rgt in the battle for Derna. As a result of what amounted to a delaying action orchestrated by Lt-Col HD Drew, the Germans were held back long enough for the other British troops in the area to escape eastward.[78]

On the 7 April, knowing that Neame and O'Connor were missing, an important meeting, took place in Cairo to discuss the parlous situation in Cyrenaica. The participants included Gen Archibald Wavell, Secretary of State for War Anthony Eden, Air Chief Marshall Sir Arthur Longmore and Admiral Sir Andrew Cunningham. That high-level conference chose Tobruk 'as the site to make the stand, in part to deny the port to the enemy ... because it was a ready water source and a large amount of stores had already been stockpiled there'.[79] Morshead was rapidly placed in charge of defence arrangements at the fortress and Lavarack replacing Neame as GOC Cyrenaican Command.

Mechili fell on 8 April, the same day as Ponath's victory at Derna, thereby solving water problems for the *Afrika Korps*. Rommel gloated:

> The capture of Mechili was a coup; the enemy had probably not reckoned on our using the route through Ben Gania or on our appearing as early as we did in front of Mechili. Their troops were taken completely by surprise and probably were deceived

> as to our true strength. Similarly our rapid advance to Derna was unexpected. It was principally our speed that accounted for this victory.[80]

Immediately, Rommel ordered Streich to strike east to Tobruk at maximum speed; it was necessary to overrun the garrison before Morshead and Lavarack could organise its defences. This entailed a night march for Ponath's troops who were described as 'dead tired' and utterly exhausted from their exceptional exertions. Meanwhile the Australians who avoided the desert by-pass outside Derna made their way as fast as they could along the coastal road to Tobruk, traversing once more in snakelike convoys 'hair-pin bends rising up to mountains'.[81]

DISASTER AT DERNA

Writing a retrospective report, Major Thomas F Cragg outlined the arrangements undertaken on 6-7 April when the battalion set out from its holding position at Barce Pass for Ain El Gazala, having passed through the 20th Australian Bde's protective screen at Timini. The order of movement was Bn HQ, HQ, B Echelon, C, B, A, D Coys, and the route to be followed was clearly detailed – 'Turn off at GIOVANNI BERTA – DESERT ROAD – MATURTBA – AIN EL GAZALA. DERNA to be avoided ... and if trouble was encountered ... make for the sea'. With the benefit of subsequent intelligence, Cragg recorded that BHQ and HQ Coy with part of B Echelon, in 25 trucks, turned off Giovanni Berta onto the Desert Road (near Martuba) while the remainder of the battalion was diverted through Derna.

Only the four rifle companies reached Tobruk, the battalion vanguard being ambushed on the desert bypass by elements of Ponath's battalion and eighteen tanks as armoured support. It has been claimed that they were guided to their fate by a German in the guise of a British provost. When the rifle companies were held up at the check-point, they avoided disaster owing to the actions of quick-thinking CSM Don Parker who allegedly shot the impostor. Consequently they took the alternative route, proceeding along the coastal road to their destination.

Lucky to escape were Lt Gavin Gemmel-Smith and 'Osty' Ostberg who had been sent back to see what happened to the rest of the convoy. Driving towards Giovanni Berta, a distance of fourteen miles, they saw traffic still moving on the Derna Road and turned around to give their report. On the way back they encountered the Anti-Tank Coy vehicles fleeing at high speed. Having been warned that the Germans were pursuing and shooting at the straying vehicles, Gemmel-Smith and Ostberg cautiously proceeded to assess the situation. With the waiting convoy again in sight, they surmised by the clouds of smoke and burning vehicles that the battalion headquarters was under attack. Turning around, they made their way back at speed to Brigade HQ where they reported the battalion's disastrous loss. Cpl NHC Collins managed to escape in his vehicle, the B Echelon kitchen truck, at the height of the battle. His lasting impression of that ambush was 'the sound of heavy rifle and Machine-Gun (MG) fire by our men and the burst of High Explosive (HE) shells among the parked vehicles' [on top of a ridge].[82]

In that brief action near Martuba the 2/15 Bn suffered a significant loss: CO Lt-Col Marlan, 2/IC Major Barton, five other officers, C of E Padre Arkell and 150 NCOs and ORs were made POWs, and the unit was deprived of its Carrier and Mortar platoons. Major R Rosier's ensuing account of the battalion's tragedy was recorded as an appended report in its war diary:

> **BARSE PASS 6 April**
>
> ... On reaching Giovani Bertha at approximately 2230 hours the column was diverted from the Coastal road to the Desert road ... moving without lights being very difficult, so much so that shortly after crossing the escarpment, ... the vehicles of the various units became mixed up.
>
> **VICINITY OF DERNA 7 April**
>
> At first light 7 April 41, at approx 0430 hrs the column commenced to move again, but it was found that the only vehicles present were those of Bn HQ, HQ Coy and one of "B" Coy and also several vehicles of 2/3 Lt AA Regt and 2/17 Bn. The other 2/15 Bn vehicles had apparently been separated during the night.
>
> The column continued towards AIN GAZALA until 0800 hrs when the CO Lt-Col RF Marlan decided to halt near the junction of the Desert Road and a track from EL MICHILI, leading towards DERNA, to enable the rest of the Bn to catch up, and for the vehicles of the 2/17 Bn to become disengaged. ....
>
> While all personnel were dispersed, enemy vehicles were sighted coming up from the direction of EL MICHILI, and these engaged Bn with Anti Tank and MG fire at about 0830 hrs, and shortly after a number of enemy tanks also arrived from the same direction. Lt-Col Marlan decided to engage the enemy and although the enemy (troops of the German *Afrika Korps*) had considerably superior fire power and weapons, they were held off until 1030 hrs – during which time several trucks and 2/3 Lt AA vehicles were hit by incendiary bombs and burnt [from under their guns]. About 1030-1100 hrs Lt-Col Marlan [assured that the wounded would

receive medical treatment and confident of rescue] decided to surrender to avoid unnecessary casualties.[83]

The Australian prisoners from the ranks were marched to Derna airfield and trucked subsequently to the Benghazi POW cage and Tripoli before being shipped to Naples. They spent the rest of the war in POW camps in Italy and Germany. The officers and their batmen were taken in a vehicle to Derna before travelling to the same locations and then to more salubrious camps for those of their rank in Europe. 'Of the 507 Australians captured during the ill-fated withdrawal from Benghazi, 163 came from the Battalion...'.[84]

Still, the Germans missed snaring the remainder of the Australian 9th Div which had passed through the 26th Australian Bde's protective screen at Timini during 7 April. Among the last to arrive at that point was the 2/13 Bn which was hotly pursued by German tanks. After leaving El Gazala, during the evening of 8/9 April, with Capt S McKewan then at the helm as the new temporary CO, the 2/15 Bn took up a defensive position astride the Tobruk-Acroma road, covering the withdrawal of the 2/13 and 2/17.[85] The days were spent digging-in amidst the blinding, swirling *khamsin*. That was really a blessing in disguise as the storm delayed the enemy's preparations for attack and gave the commanders time to take stock of the situation. The entire battalion was finally trucked to Tobruk at 0530 on Wednesday 9 April and bivouacked five miles outside. On the following day, with Major Cragg of the 2/13 assuming the position of CO, the battalion entered the inner defence perimeter of the fortress. As the expected attack did not eventuate, Capt Peek noted that they 'had a good days rest'.[86]

The Germans were reported to be advancing in force along the road from Derna and across the desert from Mechili and concentrating south-west of Acroma outside Tobruk. Extracts from Ponath's diary reveal the arduous conditions which his battalion endured while they tried to head-off the Tobruk-bound Australians, Rommel being one of the most relentless propelling factors. 'Worse sandstorm. Everything covered in sand. ... In the darkness our tanks run over nine of our motor-cyclists. We lose our way. ... Detestable march on a mine-infested track. Casualties. At 4.30 (0430) Rommel bellows and chases us forward, out of touch with the battalion across the stony desert. Only ten vehicles with us'. On reaching Tobruk, the advance section of the battalion was unable to dig-in because of the rocky soil. They spent a sleepless night in the incredibly bitter cold.[87]

Meanwhile those within the garrison, the winners of the Benghazi Handicap spent a more comfortable night despite the industry involved in restoring and improving defences. They were fed up with retreating, low in morale and knew that they would be soon under siege. Morshead informed them that there would be no retreat; they would have to stand and fight without yielding an inch. Contrary to Rommel's expectation of an easy victory and a second Dunkirk via the harbour, the Australians were itching to retaliate and about to unleash raw courage.[88]

chapter 3

TOBRUK DEFENCES

Fortuitously, because of the scattered nature of the advancing enemy in the initial stage of occupation and the onslaught of the worst *khamsin* in local memory, the disorganised Australian units were afforded thirty-six hours respite. 'By midnight of 9 April, the *storm* was so bad that when new arrivals got out of the back of the truck, each man had to hold onto the belt of the man in front of him to find a way to the barracks'.[89]

In that precious interval, before the first German probes began, the besieged were able to regroup and reorganise, making ultimate use of the substantial lull.[90] Writing in 1959, Anthony Heckstall-Smith was full of praise for those whom Rommel labelled a rabble: 'For two days while the stifling *khamsin* lashed the surface of the desert into a raging sandstorm, wearing anti-gas goggles and with handkerchiefs over their mouths, the men of the garrison laboured ceaselessly, preparing the perimeter defences'.[91] Sappers laid a minefield around the perimeter; the infantry repaired the barbed wire; sand was shovelled out of half-filled anti-tank ditches and concrete posts; gunners dug in and camouflaged their 25-pounders; and ammunition was transported to forward posts and artillery positions. Also signallers put in a marathon effort to roll out hundreds of miles of wire to link the scattered units by field telephone.[92]

Hotly pursued by a *Panzer*, the last troops entered the perimeter just as the *khamsin* started to abate at 0400 on 10 April. The 30,000 soldiers gathered therein to defend Tobruk were predominantly an Australian contingent drawn from the three brigades of the 9th Australian Div, 18 AIF Bde of the 7th Div and 2/3rd Australian Anti-Tank Rgt. British military personnel accounted for 12,000. The latter, especially those who crewed the tanks of Royal Tank Rgt and three regiments of the RHA were particularly important in the light of future events. Also as an asset to the defence of the fortress, following their brave rearguard action at Mechili, were 1,500 soldiers from the 3rd Indian Motor Bde. Within weeks, Morshead pared that unwieldy total to 23,000, keeping within the garrison only those who were indispensable to his needs.[93]

After all allocated posts were finally occupied on 10 April, the defenders would have been able to discern the inhospitable topography for the first time. The outlying area was rocky and dusty – not sandy as is widely assumed. Mixed with shrapnel, the rocks thrown up by explosions eventually proved to be more damaging than jagged metal bomb fragments alone. The troops were inside a large semi-circle which faced the harsh, vegetation-free desert. Each side of that figure ended in steep stony wadis – impassable to tanks – which ran down to the sea and formed natural barriers. Over three miles inland they could easily discern two escarpments, between 50 and 100 feet high, rising like steps in the hinterland which was crisscrossed with roads and tracks. Pertaining to motorised transport, the Derna Road entered the western perimeter and wound into and out of the harbour precinct before branching east as the Bardia Road. The motorway which was destined to play a critical part in the forthcoming battle was the El Adem Road which headed south to the airfield bearing that name. Strategic King's Cross, a name with a distinctive Anglo/Australian flavour, marked the junction of Tobruk's northern road network.[94]

Undeterred by the raging sandstorm, Lavarack and Morshead carried out a detailed examination of Tobruk defences on 9 April with Brigadiers Wooten, Murray, Godfrey and Tovell, commanders of the 18th, 20th, 24th and 26th Bdes respectively. Morshead was familiar with the terrain and defence arrangements, having examined them after the fall of the fortress to the 6th Div in January. Furthermore, thanks to Lt-Gen O'Connor, he possessed copies of the comprehensive maps entitled 'Tobruch Defences, January 1941', detailing contours, defence positions, roads, tracks, buildings and other landmarks.[95] From those sources the high ranking officers planned the defence of Tobruk. Avoiding the Italians' mistake of concentrating strength on the outer perimeter, the 9th Div strategists emphasised defence in depth. Only 7 of the 13 battalions were placed at any one time on the front line, the remainder being retained for counterattack.

John Moore, Morshead's biographer, described the layout of the fortress in which the defenders would live until October:

> [It] was based on the extensive defences prepared by the Italians when they owned the place. These ran for eight miles east of its harbour to nine miles west, giving an

chapter 4

LEAD-UP TO THE EASTER BATTLE

Its war diary recorded that the 2/15 Bn reached the position 406429, about 1¾ miles south-west of Fort Pilastrino, at 0445 on 10 April. There it dispersed in a fan-like formation facing the south-west and dug in. The imminent tank attack, about which the troops were warned, did not eventuate. At 1630 the battalion settled into another position 412425, 1¾ miles south-west from the Pilastrino-El Adem road junction and half a mile due west from the latter road.[105] About that time the severe dust storm abated, having severely curtailed vision and movement. On the next day, coinciding with the appointment of Major Cragg as CO, the battalion headquarters were moved to a building sited at 41294262, about 250 yards south–west of the junction of the Pilastrino-El Adem crossroads. A contemporary tracing indicates that the rest of the battalion then dug in commensurately northward. At 1500 on that day, D Coy, as reserve company, was moved to the rear of the battalion to provide local protection. Two hours later, as a result of constant attack on R33 (2/17 post) on the perimeter, the battalion was ordered to stand to.[106]

Although Rommel's first attack on Tobruk occurred after midday on Thursday 10 April – after the *khamsin* finally abated – D Coy's diary recorded no significant activity on the inner perimeter where the 2/15 Bn was placed in reserve. In fact the Company enjoyed a good day's rest.[107] Strangely, no mention was made of the unnecessary movement on 11 April of 16 Platoon, D Coy under Lt WH Jubb, to the 2/17 Bn position to counterattack enemy who took refuge in an adjoining ditch.[108] The entry for the following day merely noted changes in the battalion hierarchy and the return of the *khamsin* – apparently the only event worth recording. Yet others in the 9th Div had been fighting furiously for their lives and for Tobruk's future throughout that period when the 2/15 was preparing unhindered for possible last-ditch action.

Expecting to gain advantage by speed and surprise, Rommel impulsively ordered the first incursion on 10 April, the vanguard of his scattered units reaching the Derna road approach to Tobruk. That knee-jerk reaction was bound to result in failure as he had no knowledge of the defences which the Italians had established at the fortress. Further, the intelligence he received from the Luftwaffe and other sources was faulty. He frankly acknowledged that he was at a disadvantage, knowing full well that it 'was of utmost importance to the commander to have a good knowledge of the battlefield and ... of the enemy's positions on the ground'.[109] Nevertheless he considered that he could proceed under less than ideal conditions as the calibre of the foe was inferior. After all he was not expecting a determined fight from reportedly demoralised, untrained soldiers who were hell bent on evacuation by ship: he expected a walk-over. Hence Rommel arrogantly predicted that his exhausted army, which he continually harassed to advance at relentless non-stop speed, would ultimately gain an easy victory after probes identified the enemy's weak spots.

The most advanced of the *Afrika Korps* were the lead elements of Ponath's 8 Machine-Gun Bn, Reconnaissance Bn 3 and a section of the 605 Anti-tank Rgt. They came without tanks or artillery as Streich's 5th Light Div was held up at Mechili for maintenance, much against Rommel's will. Occupying positions abandoned by the Australians on 10 April – eleven miles from the fortress – the Germans' progress came to a sudden halt after the bridge on the Via Balbia (Derna road section) was blown up by sappers from 2/3 Field Coy RAE. At that point the German advance party encountered 'murderous machine-gun fire' and salvoes from 51st Field Rgt, armoured cars and the Bush Artillery. A battle ensued for most of the day, both parties firing at each other across the gaping wadi. In the midst of this conflict, Gen von Prittwitz, who had been bullied by Rommel to attack swiftly and show some decisive leadership, charged down the road in a staff car at the head of several armoured vehicles. There his progress also was abruptly stopped. Having being killed by a direct hit from an anti-tank shell, that foolhardy and much bullied senior commander became the first of the German dead at Tobruk. In sum, after encountering 'a wall of concentrated fire' over many hours, 7 German vehicles and 2 armoured cars were knocked out. The defenders lost 2 guns, 2 carriers, 2 dead and 30 were wounded.[110] To round off his day, Rommel not only came under artillery fire from El Adem as he undertook his own reconnaissance journey in his new Mammoth, but was abused soundly by Maj-Gen Streich who, following in a captured staff car, held Rommel responsible for causing von Prittwitz's death.[111]

Harrison's evaluation of the action around and about the western precinct was highly critical of Rommel's over-confidence, impatience and poor planning – each being related to his desire for self-glorification. He concluded: 'It would not be correct to describe this as a serious attack or as a major rebuff for the attackers. It was an over-optimistic, under-prepared minor effort which collapsed after the death of a commander who had been goaded into attacking without having the opportunity to do any real commanding.'[112]

Unchastened by the Prittwitz tragedy, Rommel sent Lt Wahl and four *Panzers* to similar fates during the next morning. Lying on his stomach and surveying the Fort Pilastrino precinct through binoculars, and still convinced that Tobruk was sparsely defended, he issued the order which his ADC Lt Heinz Schmidt apparently thought was foolhardy.[113] Already coming under intense fire, Rommel then led the attack in an unarmoured, open-topped car ahead of the tanks, without infantry or artillery support, vaingloriously expecting to seize Tobruk. As von Prittwitz's 15*th Panzer* Div had at last arrived at the front to supplement Streich's 5th Motorised Light Div, Rommel went on to conjure up grander plans for Good Friday 1941. Predictably, Lt-Col Olbrich's 5th *Panzer* Rgt and Lt-Col Ponath's 8 Machine-Gun Bn, essential components of the Streich group, would continue to form the nucleus of his planning.

GOOD FRIDAY 11 APRIL 1941

Although 11 April heralded Rommel's first major attack on besieged Tobruk, involving substantial artillery action from the west of El Adem road, the 2/15 Bn near the King's Cross vicinity was relatively unaffected. Even when 16 platoon D Coy under Lt W Jubb was ordered to move to 2/17 Bn at midnight to counter enemy attack in a nearby ditch, they were not used – the enemy had been dislodged before they arrived.[114]

Rommel was at the Tobruk front throughout the action on 11 April, directing operations by conveying messages to the spearhead.[115] His second and more determined attempt to breach Tobruk's defences took place about 1500hrs around the ten-mile southern sector held by Brig John Murray's 20th Bde – the reserve battalion's parent body. While the Italian Brescia Div attacked in the west as diversion, Olbrich's tried and true *Panzers* and Pontath's dependable infantry, reinforced by two companies of the 605th Anti-tank Bn, assaulted the perimeter west of El Adem road. Their objective was the area between outposts R33 and R35 which was defended by elements of the 2/17 Bn. Lyman outlined Rommel's strategy: 'Once Ponath's infantry had made an opening in the wire, suppressed the defences and cleared the area of mines, Olbrich's tanks would pour through the breach, fanning out left and right along the perimeter to roll up the Australian positions from the flank'.[116]

At 1500, Olbrich's men, arriving at the designated point where they linked up with the 8 Machine-Gun Bn, came straight away under constant artillery fire 400 yards from the posts of the 2/13. The Panzers and troops, easy targets for the RHA's white-hot 25-pounders, advanced through a relatively ineffective barrage of Brens, rifles, grenades and a few Boys anti-tank rifles towards D Coy, 2/17 Bn. After encountering the anti-tank ditch of variable depth, Olbrich opened up on forward posts before turning his squadron right and drove along the edge of the ditch along the 2/17's front, in search of an entry.

Meanwhile the infantry, 700 in number and shoulder to shoulder, moved forward in bounds under the cover of their machine guns to reach the anti-tank ditch from which they mortared adjoining posts. The 70 accompanying tanks, on encountering the unexpected anti-tank ditch, the recently laid minefield and unpredicted infantry resistance, moved along the ditch – the 2/13's perimeter. Unsuccessful in locating a crossing for both tanks and troops, Olbrich lost 4 vehicles after a confrontation with 11 cruisers which emerged from the perimeter defences. Lyman confided that there was no escape from the RAF: 'Olbrich's tanks were hit by Bristol Blenheims, flying out of Egypt, and Hurricanes from El Gubbi launched attacks on vehicles moving along El Adem road, machine gunning them from 50 feet'.[117] Meanwhile the British artillery bombarded and the RAF Hurricanes of 73 Squadron strafed Ponath's isolated machine-gunners whose casualties consequently amounted to 44 dead and wounded.[118]

That extended probe by the *Panzers* deprived the 8 Machine-Gun Bn of its tank support and therefore left it in a most vulnerable position. Harassed by strafing attacks and murderous machine-gun fire, Ponath's men were eventually expelled from their foothold in the ditch by a fierce Australian counterattack. As the infantry's advance had been stopped, the Germans were isolated and open to the unerring aim of snipers and unremitting machine-gun fire. Unable to dig foxholes, they ultimately resorted to scraping out a line of rough and ready shallow trenches from rock and sand with trenching tools, hands, bayonets and helmets to secure a modicum of uneasy protection. These infantrymen, coming under both artillery and small arms fire and not daring to move even slightly, remained pinned down, 400 yards from the ditch. With orders to maintain their gains, Ponath's infantry stayed put, eventually being discovered there at first light on Easter Saturday by the 2/17 after the welcome respite accompanying nightfall.[119]

An analysis of the siege of Tobruk was written in 1986 by Col Ward A Miller of the US Army and General Command Staff College for officers at the College's Combat Studies Institute. He considered that the Australians' defence of Tobruk was a classic example of successful infantry defence against tanks. He summarised the first of two ensuing battles as follows:

> ... the 1st Royal Tank Regiment with its eleven cruiser tanks moved up in the direction of the El Adem roadblock. After skirting the 2/17's front, the enemy tanks moved along the 2/13's perimeter, firing to suppress the forward posts as they passed. Along the El Adem road, gunners of the 2/13's mortar platoon, manning two Italian 47-mm anti-tank guns, knocked out one Italian medium tank and hit several others. Another Italian light tank, disabled by small–arms fire, was knocked out by one of the anti-tank guns and its crew was captured.
>
> At the El Adem road, enemy tanks halted before a minefield and turned away just as the 1st Royal Tank Regiment arrived. Both sides engaged at long range. Three light tanks and one medium Italian tank were knocked out by British tanks and one German medium tank was destroyed by anti-tank fire. Two British medium tanks were lost. The enemy withdrew south, having lost seven tanks.[120]

Initiating the first of Morshead's aggressive patrols beyond the perimeter, combat troops from the 2/17's reserve company found that the enemy had withdrawn from the anti-tank ditch in front of D Coy. Also detected was a group of pioneers from Engineers Bn 200 who specialised in the penetration of defences. Equipped with demolitions and Bangalore torpedoes, they apparently intended cutting through the protecting wire and bridging the anti-tank ditch. That breaching party, leaving behind its lethal equipment, was easily driven off by an Australian patrol. Later that night, further probes by *Panzers* occurred along the ditch in front of the 2/13. Thus the writing was on the wall: the Germans would attack the south-eastern sector held by the 20th and 24th Bdes at dawn on the 12th. To that end, parties of Australian troops laboured feverishly throughout the evening to sow thousands of mines along the front of the threatened battalions.

EASTER SATURDAY 12 APRIL 1941

According to the war diaries of D Coy and the battalion, all remained quiet around King's Cross; however, both recorded the heavy dust storm which caused the troops to suffer from 'eyesore' and strain. Undoubtedly they were busy improving their defences while the British artillery was fully occupied propelling shells by the hundred to the front.

Morshead ordered the four batteries of 25-pounder guns from 1RHA to be dug in just south of the junction of the El Adem and Bardia roads to provide fire support and act as a back-up position. Three of the 2/15's companies were relocated in front of those batteries, his two other reserve battalions being disposed at Fort Airente and Fort Pilastrino. Also moved up to the King's Cross area were several 2-pounder portees from 3RHA and weapons of the 2/3 Australian Anti-Tank Rgt. Further, Lt-Col Drew, commander of the 5th RTR was warned to be ready for an enemy attack in this vicinity. Completing a water-tight ambush strategy, Morshead also planned to call in Bristol Blenheims from RAF bases in Egypt to attack German vehicle clusters.[121]

The whole garrison stood to arms on Easter Saturday morning, but the anticipated assault did not happen. Regardless, the enemy dug in about 400 yards in front of Capt JW Balfe's company from where it brought sniping, mortar and machine-gun fire to bear upon the 2/17's perimeter. Eventually the guns were engaged and silenced by Bren Gun fire.

Some tanks appeared in front of the 2/17 Bn looking for gaps in the anti-tank ditch. One concentration of vehicles was heavily shelled for 1½ hours by 1RHA while three Blenheim bombers took care of another. Under the cover of the *khamsin*, the German infantry advanced on Posts R33 and R35, but were temporarily brought to ground 500 yards from the perimeter by fire from both troops of the B/O Battery of 1RHA. When they resumed their advance after an hour, the battery broke up the attack, systematically shelling their flanks and then their centre. While most took shelter in the anti-tank ditch, one group embarked upon a fire fight with reinforcements manning R33. After 6 RAF bombers attacked 60 vehicles, including tanks, near El Adem road, the greater part of the German infantry retired to a position 1500 yards from the perimeter.[122] Up to that point, the German forces, lacking a significant artillery component, had made no impression on overcoming Australian defences.

Rommel, who was planning a fourth attempt to break through Tobruk's defences on Easter Sunday, was handicapped by his troops' exhaustion after ten days of concentrated action, inadequate victualling and vehicles in want of urgent repair. This time, he possessed an invaluable Italian map of Tobruk's defences to draw up a realistic assault strategy for the following day:

> The plan required that the 5th *Light Division* should make a breach in the perimeter defences on the evening of the 13th and penetrate to the junction of the Bardia and El Adem Roads while the *Brescia Division* staged a demonstration in the west to pin down the forces there. In the early hours of the next morning the main force would thrust through the bridgehead to launch at dawn an attack towards the harbour.[123]

EASTER SUNDAY 13 APRIL 1941

Major Cragg reported in the battalion diary that 13 April 1941 was generally quiet, although just before midnight, D Coy was called upon to act as a counterattack force: the action associated with this move was to be played out in the early hours of the next morning. Yet the brigade diary noted that an infantry attack which was supported by tanks developed on the fronts of the 2/13 and 2/17 Bns was dispersed by artillery fire. Obviously the perimeter held by those battalions was the focus of Rommel's close attention and thus it was in this region that the Tobruk drama unfolded.[124]

The onslaught had been preceded by a leaflet drop from the Luftwaffe over the whole garrison, requesting wholesale British surrender by display of white handkerchiefs. Summarily rebuffing the demand, Morshead wryly indicated that the garrison was unable to comply because of the shortage of anything resembling white rags within the dusty, water-scarce perimeter.[125] Probably the General Officer Commanding the German Forces in Libya, if he had access to the response, would have grasped its cryptic intent – that no cowards would be found among Tobruk's defenders.

The advent of dawn revealed motorcyclists followed by a staff car 2000 yards out from 2/17 Bn's front – presumably the nucleus of a German headquarters. More trucks drove up to the perimeter of the eastern and western sectors in mid-afternoon, resulting in the capture of several German prisoners and trucks of British origin. Incredibly, given the deception played out on the 2/15's HQ in the vicinity of Derna, one vehicle contained two motorcycles and an Australian and an Indian uniform.[126]

Rommel was making preparations to storm the fortress. While armoured cars surveyed the southern perimeter, lorries unloaded troops about 4000 yards away. After British artillery dispersed that concentration, small detachments were brought forward to positions 1500 yards out. There they installed machine guns to strafe perimeter posts, especially those of the 2/17tth Bn.[127]

Meanwhile most of Ponath's troops were still holding their positions in make-shift shelters or sangars outside the perimeter, unable to move across open ground and subject to heavy artillery and infantry fire. They had been in action for an unbroken fortnight, desperately in need of rest. Having received orders to report to Rommel's headquarters, Ponath managed to crawl unscathed to and from that location in the afternoon, returning completely exhausted to his exposed position with new attack plans. As Harrison explained: 'He and his men were to attempt what Olbrich [the tanks] had failed to do. Under the cover of darkness, they were to get over the ditch, cross the wire and open up a gap through which the Panzers could advance'.[128]

Given the superiority of the German radio communications system and knowing that German decorations were habitually revealed in the field, Rommel probably also informed Ponath that he had been awarded Germany's highest military decoration – the Knights Cross of the Iron Cross. It had been announced that day in Berlin and probably telegraphed immediately to the front: he would be decorated for his exemplary action in Cyrenaica.[129]

In a letter to his wife Lucie, written on 13 April, Rommel complained that the 5th Light Div had not mastered the art of concentrating its strength at one point, forcing a break-through, rolling up and securing the flank on either side and then penetrating like lightning before the enemy had time to react, 'deep in his rear'. Consequently he was putting his faith in Ponath to show the rest of his army how the job should be done. At 1800hrs the Machine-Gun Bn under the Ponath's leadership would begin its raid, demolishing the anti-tank ditch and breaking through the British defences to create a bridgehead from which the next day's attack could be launched.[130]

'With uncanny foresight', Morshead predicted that the attack would occur on the 2/17's front. Therefore he dug in four batteries of 1RHA's 25-pounders to cover the endangered sector while the portees of 3RHA and anti-tank guns of 3AAT were placed near King's Cross and another six of 3RHA's anti-tank guns were located at the posts most at risk. Hence Rommel personally directed the artillery assault on R31 and R32 and infantry attack on R33 which occurred at 1700hrs. While the latter was driven back by small-arms fire, the former was kept in check by the four batteries of 1RHA. When the huge 88mm guns were brought into action, their crews were quickly massacred as were those manning the 22mm guns who attempted to attack the Australian infantry from the ditch.[131]

Ponath reported he was under such heavy artillery fire that he was unable to move. Hence an attack across open ground under such conditions was impossible. Nevertheless, during the evening, his troops crossed the ditch and dealt with the many mines to settle in a better position where they could keep the Australians under surveillance. 'Ponath, with a party of forty – his *Panzergrenadiers* and pioneers from Pioneer Bn 200 – made the crossing, 100 yards east of R33 and immediately brought their weapons into action against it'.[132] He was amazed at the scant resistance they encountered. In the process his sappers carefully cleared away the barbed wire and unearthed the mines which they neatly stacked on either side of the proposed opening. Unwittingly Ponath chose a point for the breach between two perimeter strong points, but with more luck the tank ditch of that sector had a depth of only 2ft 6ins and foundations of solid rock.[133] Having gained this foothold in the perimeter at 2300hrs, Ponath decided to shut down the defences at R33 before opening up the breach through which the *Panzers* could advance. Hence a party of 30 infantrymen with 2 small field guns, 1 mortar and 8 machine-guns dug in 100 yards to the east of R33 and directed fire on that vital post.[134]

In turn, the commander of that beleaguered post, Lt FA Mackell, having directed fire unsuccessfully against the intruders, decided to mount a counterattack during the first hour of the next day. By such action, he intended to quell the enemy's assault and to dislodge it from its critical foothold. Predictably, there ensured a bitter fight between Ponath's well-equipped *Panzergrenadiers* and Mackell's small party of aggressive Australian invaders.

chapter 5

THE EASTER BATTLE FOR TOBRUK

EASTER MONDAY 14 APRIL 1941

Easter Monday 14 April was the critical day in the battle for Tobruk. It was heralded by a fierce, hand-to-hand battle between an Australian raiding party, made up of Mackell and five men from Cpl Jack Edmonston's section, and the German intruders. Under the cover of machine-gun fire directed on the German post by troops at Post R33, the Australians attacked the German flank. Coming under fierce fire themselves, they attacked the Germans with grenades, rifles fired from the hip and bayonet. The ferocity of the Australians caused most of the Germans to flee in terror, leaving their arms and equipment behind. Nevertheless some, including their badly wounded leader, Captain Frank, put up a brave resistance. While the Germans lost a dozen men as well as one captured, the 2/17 Battalion suffered the death of Cpl Edmonston who, despite machine-gun inflicted wounds to stomach and neck, fought bravely until the last of the enemy was evicted. Saving the life of his platoon commander in the height of the conflict, he alone accounted for at least seven of the enemy dead. After being carried back to R33, he died there before medical aid could be sought. Subsequently, he was posthumously awarded the Victoria Cross for his courage and self-sacrifice: the first Australian VC winner of World War II.[135]

Maughan has highlighted the role of the forward posts in keeping the perimeter gaps under steady fire, operating in conjunction with the second line posts which covered the ground in between. The deadly aim of snipers like Bob Scarr, who attracted begrudging admiration from the Germans, and fire from the posts also eliminated several anti-tank gun crews and machine-gunners. Such pro-activity ensured the mammoth 88mm field piece, as well as the lesser field guns, became inoperable, thereby guaranteeing that scant support was available to tanks or infantry on arrival or during advance.[136]

At 0215, 200 men from the 8 Machine-Gun Bn, undeterred by fire from R33 and an artillery barrage from two RHA batteries, returned to their foothold and set about extending their penetration into Australian positions. Laying down 'heavy suppressive fire' on that post and its western counterparts, the large contingent ensured that the engineers from Pioneer Bn 200 finished the mine-freed passage across the anti-tank ditch unhindered. Eventually Lt-Col Ponath led his troops across the ditch, dug in behind R33 and established a beachhead. Once more, shelled and under heavy small arms fire from neighbouring posts, the Germans stayed put within the perimeter despite heavy casualties.

Following Morshead's directive to the letter, the Australian infantry manning the forward posts lay low in their gun pits, letting the *Panzers* advance over the top of their lairs. Then, when the coast was clear, they arose from their pits, took up their .303s and Brens to take care of the unaware German infantry following behind or perched upon their terrifying tanks.

The Australian resistance ultimately forced the 8 Machine-Gun Bn to advance towards Tobruk with only 200 men, 100 others being committed to holding the beachhead. On the other hand, the strength and determination of the Germans in attack resulted in Captain E Peek's D Coy, 2/15 Bn, being deployed as a back-up force at the rear of Captain Balfe's harassed D Coy 2/17 Bn. Unhindered, Ponath's men, nearly two companies in strength, fanned out and proceeded two miles northwards towards the El Adem crossroads where they were expecting to rendezvous with the thirty-eight tanks of Olbrich's 5th Armoured Regiments. As in Europe, the *Panzers* were expected to roll on and take Tobruk with ease. The German infantry fully expected to chase and destroy the Australian reserve 2/15 Bn, which was dug in around 1RHA's 25-pounders about a quarter of a mile south-west of the El Adem / Palastrino roads junction, as its troops broke ranks and fled westward from the *Panzers.*

Evidently, the only company under Ponath's command – the right hand flank of the advance party – made it relatively unscathed to the King's Cross precinct as they attempted 'to broaden the gap in the perimeter and secure the flanks'. Concentrated artillery fire barrages from the north and small-arms fire from behind most likely caused many from the other half of the forward party – those on the left flank – to seek refuge in scattered hollows and principally in Goshen's house not far from R32.

Captain Balfe, Company Commander within the 2/17 Bn, had observed Ponath's infantry advancing in fan-out formation. Being frustrated by the bridgehead and then being temporarily hemmed in by the *Panzer* incursion, he took the unprecedented step of ordering the RHA to fire on his own position.[137]

PURSUING THE PANZER

As Percy Lyall of D Coy noted, it was A Coy which first saw action within the 2/15 Bn during the Easter conflict, the major tank battle with the RHA taking place on its front. Unaware of the calibre of the leadership and the bravery of the unwavering NCOs – many of officer potential – and those in the ranks from the rough and tough western Queensland area, the Germans' expectations could not have been further from the reality they ultimately experienced. Led by injured and unarmed Captain Greig Smith and backed by Lts Ron Yates, Bill Cobb and Lance Bode – subsequently each a Military Cross winner – A Coy ensured that the formerly undefeated 8 Machine-Gun Bn would undergo action against a formidable foe, the likes of which it had never encountered before. There were three other companies of similar quality to deal with, making the 2/15 Bn a quintessential exemplar of Morshead's unyielding ideal.

At 0520 the first German tanks entered the perimeter through the gap near R33 and unwittingly headed for Balfe's headquarters at R32, about half a mile inside the wire. There the *Panzers* passed by the defensive posts and grouped together, ready to progress when all arrived at the designated assembly spot. The first wave of 15 tanks towed anti-tank guns and each subsequent vehicle came under artillery fire which the RHA directed accurately on that position. Eventually Lt-Col Olbrich's lead battalion of the 15th Tank Regiment of 38 vehicles assembled three-quarters of a mile inside the perimeter wire, taking aboard members of Ponath's infantry. The second battalion eventually caught up and followed close behind as support. They were in high expectation of yet another 'pushover' four miles north at the El Adem crossroads. With the mechanised troops, the *Panzers* would pour through the gap, 'fan out behind the defences and roll them up.'[138] As the attack was following the same pattern as all the other German attacks which proved to be invincible in Europe, German confidence ran high.

The Brigade War Diary reveals that an attack was launched at 0550 on 2/17 Bn front, lorried German infantry being preceded by 40 tanks entered the perimeter. After being strongly attacked by 2/17 Bn, the enemy was routed and withdrew. German losses were considerable, 100 being killed and 10 officers and 257 ORs being taken prisoner.[139]

Perc Lyall was generous with his praise of his 2/17 D Coy counterparts who put into practice Morshead's infantry tactics which required the troops to remain unobtrusive to the tanks while engaging the following infantry. He recalled that 'the coy lay in their pits to allow the German tanks to roll over them and the Germans were unaware of the presence of this line, so they rolled on into a killing field commanded by our 25-pounders (RHA).'[140] In the more formal style of an accomplished historian, Maughan outlined the enemy's invariable infantry-tank transport arrangements upon which Morshead relied to diminish infantry strength:

> ... 15 or 20 men followed each tank or rode on it, but dropped behind once they were within the perimeter. ... The enemy machine-gun crews who had been riding on the tanks were mostly killed or wounded; the tanks moving on without them, while the accompanying infantry scattered or moved back towards the wire and, for the most part disorganised were engaged from the posts.[141]

The unsupported *Panzers* also unsuspectingly ran into a trap. They proceeded slowly along a corridor of artillery, anti-tank guns and tanks as they moved towards their objective. 'Ahead of them were the 25-pounders of the 1st RHA and the anti-tank guns of the 3rd Australian Regiment. To their left were the mobile anti-tank guns of the 3rd RHA, and to their right more mobile guns of the same regiment, as well as cruiser tanks of the 1st Royal Tank regiment.'[142] Without the support of their anti-tank and field guns and the majority of the 8 Machine-Gun Bn – all severely mauled by the Australian infantry – the *Panzers* had little hope of breaking through the solid defences provided by the British artillery and Australian infantry which were dug down behind the emergent Blue Line.[143] Obviously that thin blue line was protected by the 2/15 Battalion, spread out in a south westerly direction, one mile below the El Adem-Pilastrino road junction. The companies were entrenched 200 yards in front of the RHA, A Company's HQ being 70 yards to the rear of A/E Battery.[144]

With the noise of shelling intensifying on and around the permitter, Captain Greig Smith ordered A Coy to 'stand to' and be ready to fight at 2am. At that juncture he outlined to his company, Morshead's plan of attack, designed to separate the German tanks from their infantry protection. Much of the ensuing resolve and steadfastness shown by that group of Queenslanders has since been attributed to the steadying influence of Capt Smith who readied his company of young men for their first taste of battle.[145]

Five hours of suspense and waiting elapsed before daylight and improved visibility revealed a detachment of at least 25 advancing tanks manoeuvring 1,000 yards in front of the Coy's position and behind 2/17's defensive position. Look-out Cpl Jack Anning, who alerted Smith as ordered, recalled that those tanks advanced in columns of ten, the infantry running behind or riding on the iron-clad, heavily armoured vehicles.[146] Looking at the same scene, 19 year old Gordon Wallace was overawed by the enormous size of the *Panzers,* still describing them as 'big bastards' seventy years later in an Australia-wide interview.[147]

When it was established that the tanks were German, immediate preparations were made to engage the enemy by the RHA's 4 x 25-pounders which they nicknamed *Ratsch-booms* because of the sound they made. Incongruously, Smith saw this as a chance to put his mortar skills to the test, having been the battalion's mortar officer before he managed to escape the ambush of his platoon at Derna. Demonstrating that the officers shared some of the troops' irreverence, he asked the RHA to hold fire while he and Lt Cobb, his company's 2/1C, 'had a crack' at the enemy with a 2 -inch mortar at 200 to 300 yards. After they fired two shots, the first landing in front of the leading tank and the second behind, they asked the RHA battery to proceed.[148] A Coy HQ, situated close behind one ill-fated gun of A/E Battery, obviously enjoyed a strongly forged relationship with the RHA which emerged with distinction in the thick of the ensuing battle.

The small mortar party had probably been encouraged by the OCs of the 2/9, the reserve battalion which was assigned to continue action if the 2/15 was overrun by the Germans. Among that group which turned up to witness the tank battle and the ensuing mop-up action from the best vantage point – elevated A Coy HQ – was Capt Ossie Condon, one of Capt Smith's Commonwealth Bank colleagues from Brisbane. Condon, according to Smith's recollection, 'appeared like Tom Mix' toting two revolvers slung low from his hips. Hence one of Condon's first observations was that his friend had neither a revolver nor binoculars and was in a severely injured state.[149] Having come off second best to a Stuka's bomb on the previous day in a truck, when passing its real target, an abandoned Italian munition dump, Smith exhibited signs of serious spinal injuries viz. a paralysed left arm and shoulder with an acute neck injury. With orders from Battalion HQ not to enter the field but to stay continuously by the phone ('that bloody phone'), Smith led his Coy courageously and contributed significantly to his battalion's and brigade's effort to inflict the first defeat of German troops in the Second World War.[150] According to the letters which Lt Ron Yates wrote home, it took nearly three months to persuade 'that ordinary bloke ... one of the most honest men I have met ... a fellow who would not do you a bad turn if he tried...' to enter Kantara Hospital for treatment.[151] He didn't want to let the side down.

A and B Companies guarded E and Chestnut Troops of A/E Battery of 1 RHA respectively, each troop comprising four 25-pounder cannon. C Company was situated to the left and D Company placed behind as reserve. They were dug in astride the *Panzers'* projected route of advance on high ground between the Pilastrino escarpment and Sid Mahmud, being so sited that the enemy tanks would run straight into the guns after emerging from a funnelling gulley. The opening phase of the artillery battle was officially recorded: 'The first shot from No1 gun set the leading tank on fire. No2's first shot lifted the turret clean off another tank – there were soon 15 or more tanks firing at us with 75mm and 37mm cannon and machine guns....'[152]

RSM Reg Batten of 1RHA described the advance of the *Panzers* with the inexorable, steady, loping pace of a surreal leviathan:

> So long as they were a mile away we couldn't stop them because they were so well dispersed. They kept their machine guns going as they moved, but when the Mark IVs used their big "75", they stopped, took deliberate aim at our flashes and came on again. They seemed to work to a plan. Some fired while some kept moving. The bulk of their tanks headed straight for the gap between two troops of our guns, but the two Mark IVs tried to go round our flank ...[153]

Chester Wilmots' assertion that the German tanks were stopped 600 yards from the British artillery is wide of the mark. The 25-pounders were sited about 1000 yards west of the Palistrino-El Adem intersection and on a hill 300 yards below this route. The experience of Sgt Major Kevin Robinson in the trenches with 8 Platoon and Cpl Jack Anning with 9 Platoon, revealed that *Panzers* in fact reached the Australian lines (mostly 200 yards in front of the RHA); one even breaking through. Cpl Anning recalled that a German tank crossed the corner of one of 9 Platoon's weapon pits, causing him to fall flat on his face lest he be killed. However, the progress of that mighty mammoth was short lived; while proceeding apace towards the RHA emplacements, it was taken out by a 25-pounder at point-blank range.[154]

The German tanks and Ponath's depleted infantry bore the brunt of enormous fire from the Australian riflemen and British artillery which were shooting with lethal effect over open sights.[155] During 20 minutes of action, the two artillery troops had fired over 100 rounds, but unfortunately two of their guns were knocked out and 10 men were killed. RSM Batten remarked that the scene resembled Blackpool illuminations, the artillery shells, machine-gun rounds and tracer bullets filling the air with cordite and colour – not to mention the dog fights involving RAF Hurricanes and Messerschmitts above. Similarly, Lt Joachim Schorm, *Panzer* commander, likened the red hot reception he received to a 'witch's cauldron.'[156]

CSM Robinson noted the ordered manner in which about 10 tanks advanced in line formation, firing their guns ceaselessly. After the fourth tank in line was hit, halting the others following it, the first three continued their progress forward. Ultimately they reached thirty yards from the front of 8 Platoon, stopping in front of a dummy minefield of aerial bombs laid by the Italians. 8 Platoon kept up a constant barrage on the tanks, even firing down the barrels of the *Panzers'* cannon.

Cpl Jack Anning, of 9 Platoon, was elated that either he or Pte Bob Scarr, A Coy's other sniper, scored a direct hit through a chink in the armour of one of the leading *Panzers,* obviously wounding or killing its driver. The rudderless tank careered out of control, colliding with the following tanks which retreated in disarray. Yet, amidst that turmoil, there was an amusing interlude. Cheering loudly, some excited infantrymen climbed from their pits when they saw the Second Panzer regiment collide with the following First Panzer Regiment. However this show of spontaneity was not appreciated by RHA personnel who told the A Coy cheer squad to return to their trenches post haste if they valued their lives as the artillery was firing behind them hull down.[157]

Realising the rest of the squadron with the remnants of 8 Machine-Gun Bn had long departed with their wounded from a hell hole, the three lead tanks turned around and joined the rest which had retired in retreat 1,000 yards away. In a long ditch nearby, after taking some of the wounded aboard, the *Panzers* deposited the German commander and his intact men – approximately a company in number. As the *Panzers* were milling around in groups, they presented easy targets to the RHA which proceeded to knock out another four.[158]

Maughan gives full credit to A/E Battery for turning the assault around, contesting the relentless enemy advance for over three-quarters of an hour. The artillerymen stood by their guns and 'prov[ed] more steadfast than the enemy.'[159] Anning was amazed at the teamwork and the efiiciency of the British artillerymen who fired off shells in rapid succession with the precision, co-ordination and speed that could only be equalled by well-oiled machines. Equally impressed was Cpl Gordon Wallace who described the attacking skills of the artillerymen in the Chestnut battery as 'magnificent'.[160]

Recognition is also due to the 2/15 Bn's infantry, particularly those of A and B Coys who stood firm, being dug in 200 yards in front of the British artillery. Dodging enemy machine-gun and cannon fire, often delivered from a distance not much longer than a cricket pitch, some of the infantry made the lot of the *Panzer* crews just as dangerous by their well-aimed, rapid-fire shooting. Adhering to Morshead's plan, most stood firm, ready to deal with the shielded enemy infantry after the tanks passed through.

The victory was not achieved without severe losses to 1RHA. In the Chestnut group, 5 men were killed and 3 wounded. E Troop suffered the loss of five killed and one seriously wounded. Adjoining A Coy HQ, that troop also lost its No1 gun and all its crew from a direct hit from a 75mm shell when it engaged *Panzers* which were attempting to outflank the guns. Demonstrating the bravery and resolve of the RHA, RSM Batten managed to get a volley away from another E Troop weapon despite severe wounds and the death of his crew. He recounted:

> We were about to fire again when a 75mm shell hit us square on the shield. The gun was knocked out and all the crew, except myself, were either killed or wounded. I managed to fire the round that was still in the gun and the tanks turned tail and withdrew. It was good that they didn't know that we couldn't fire again and that no other gun nearby could have tackled them if they kept going. But they turned back and later the tank we hit lost its track.[161]

The fact that the two guns knocked out with heavy casualties were under the protection of A Coy, highlights the bravery and steadfastness of those Queensland troops who underwent their first baptism of fire from a formidable foe who threatened them from virtually arms length. Those based in the posts around A Coy HQ, which was situated some 70 yards behind a completely destroyed artillery piece, deserve commendation. Just as those troops in fixed forward defensive positions feared a shot that fell short from the artillery at their rear, those in the rear defences were highly anxious about receiving a round that overshot its target.

The Queensland infantry took the full brunt of all that the legendary German victors could throw at them. It was a fact that the best armies of Britain, France and Poland, when faced with the same situation, chose to flee. But the Queenslanders held fast along with the RHA, dealing out significant discomfort to their attackers, most adhering to Morshead's injunction to the letter. The 20th Brigade War Diary recorded that the Panzer attack was defeated principally because 'our men held their positions after enemy tanks had penetrated behind them.'[162] The Queensland 2/15 Bn, which stood firm as the *Panzers* threatened to progress forward, could thereafter hold its head high in the company of its equally brave southern counterparts, the 2/13 and 2/17 Bns. More importantly, it could claim, and should have been accorded, a valid position of importance in the siege's history.

The fleeing *Panzer* endured a most hazardous trip back to the perimeter. On turning east they ran into fire from the two guns of the 3rd Australian ATR which claimed to have knocked out four *Panzers*, having caught them enfilade. Then they came under frontal fire from the 25-pounders of B/O Battery of 1RHA which was situated on the north-eastern side of El Adem road, below the Bardia road offshoot. Unfortunately in the ensuing lethal duel, Rocket Troop of that unit lost three guns and suffered the deaths of many men. Having escaped that barrage, the Germans then were harassed on both flanks by the mobile anti-tank guns, mounted on 30 cwt trucks, of J Battery, 3RHA. They were then engaged and pursued to the perimeter by British cruisers. Four miles south of the area designated for the Blue Line, the enemy tanks regrouped for another attack, but the constant shelling from the guns deterred them. Further, the lack of anti-tank field guns and support from the retired 8 Machine-Gun Rgt rendered the situation hopeless. While the German tanks were being engaged simultaneously by everything Morshead could throw at them in that final phase of the battle, eight German tanks were knocked out by anti-tank and field guns, taking the total German *Panzer* losses for the battle to 17.

Contributing to the German's hell at Tobruk, spectacular dog-fights took place above the field of conflict. 'Hurricanes were fighting an unequal battle with German and Italian fighters.'[163] Ironically, it was a dangerous assignment for the low-flying Australian airmen who tried to drive off the pursuing Luftwaffe while traversing this battleground. They not only had to avoid the fire from Messershmitts on their tails, but also the anti-aircraft salvos from their trench-bound compatriots. This proved to be a fatal situation for Pilot Officer KK Jones of 3 Squadron, RAAF who was caught up in the latter while trying to shake off enemy planes. The source of his demise was an Italian 20mm anti-aircraft gun which 11 Platoon, B Coy operated enthusiastically and usually inaccurately during German air attacks.[164]

By 0730, with the Germans in full retreat, 40 Ju-87 dive bombers (Stukas) ironically arrived to bomb Tobruk harbour as the final phase of Rommel's strategy, synchronised to coincide with expected German victory at El Adem crossroads. HQ 20 Bde reported that while twelve German planes were brought down, the RAF lost two aircraft.[165]

Meanwhile enemy tanks and infantry were jostling each other to escape through the perimeter to the safety of the desert beyond. Lt Schrom, German tank officer, described that panic-stricken exit through the 'witch's cauldron':

> Close in and on our right flanks the English tanks shoot into our midst. We are struck in the tracks which creak and groan. Everything hastens towards it [the gap]. English anti-tank guns shoot into the mass. Our own anti-tank and .88mm anti-aircraft guns are almost deserted. The crews are lying silently beside them. Italian artillery which was to have protected our left flank is equally deserted. We go on. Now comes the gap. Now the ditch. The driver cannot see a thing for the dust... The tank almost gets stuck in the two ditches but manages to extricate itself after a great struggle. With their last reserves of power the crew get out of range and we return to camp ... We were lucky to escape alive.[166]

INTERCEPTING THE INFANTRY

Taking a leaf from Ponath's brief, the Australians wanted to pursue the German infantry into the desert and destroy them. However, the subsequent refusal to allow this action may have been unsound. Having lost 45% of their tanks and the greater part of the 8 Machine-Gun Bn, the Germans faced the possibility that their severely depleted infantry within the perimeter could be annihilated. They were caught in a trap. If they took the option of flight, they were threatened with the near certainty of being eradicated at the breach. If they hid within the perimeter in wadis or depressions, as many did, they would be certainly mopped up. In that case, they took the chance of ending up as POWs or corpses, depending on the make-up of the hunting party. After putting the enemy tanks to flight, the Australians could have inflicted a near-terminal blow upon the *Afrika Korps* if they had done a Ponath and mopped up the fleeing Germans.

Thus Morshead ordered counter-attacks against the pockets of German infantry within the perimeter and those ensconced at the rear of the perimeter posts holding onto the bridgehead. Long sweeps by Australians wielding bayonets and lobbing grenades ensued. Lyman noted that the 2/15 and 2/17 Battalions undertook the two major mopping up operations between King's Cross and the perimeter for the remainder of the morning. D Coy 2/15 Bn, which had previously acted as a back-up Coy to D Coy 2/17 Bn, was briefly involved in one of the southern raids.[167]

Nearly 100 of Ponath's *Panzergrenadiers* were established on a reverse slope behind Goshen's house, near Balfe's D Coy HQ (Post 32). Assisted by the containing action of Capt Peek's Coy (deployed behind D Coy 2/17), Capt CH Wilson, OC of B Coy 2/17 Bn, led a platoon in an attack on that large group. Consequently, 75 Germans from Ponath's battalion were captured, and a handful killed. The remainder escaped to establish pockets which would be cleared inevitably.[168] At 0820, D Coy 2/15 Bn was despatched to relieve its 2/17 Bn counterpart, taking over posts 29 to 35 after prisoners had been rounded up. No casualties were incurred in the process.[169] By 0830, apart from having to deal with a small number of individuals, mopping-up had been completed in the southern sector. There remained to be subdued one more large concentration of Ponath's infantrymen, holding out in the north. This action took place half an hour later.

At 0810, when A Coy front was clear except for burning tanks and planes, and the dust and smoke had subsided, RHA reported to CSM Robinson that they had seen men getting into a half-dug anti-tank ditch in the vicinity of some disabled tanks: apparently they were trying to get them restarted.[170] Impressed by their courage, Snipers Scarr and Anning, decided to spare the frustrated 'mechanics'.

As the machine-gun bursts from the tanks had long ceased, the Australians got out of their pits and, standing on the surrounding sandbags, scanned the German tank area. Robinson, with the only pair of binoculars in the Company, made out twelve to fifteen members of the German tank crews running for cover in the ditch. As the ten intact German tanks were just leaving for the southern perimeter 'hell-hole', the RHA's 25-pounders were still firing in the precinct to see them on their way. After reporting the incident to Captain Greig Smith, OC of A Coy, permission was sought from Battalion HQ for Lt Ron Yates of 9 platoon, with Robinson as guide, to try to clear the enemy troops from the area.

According to Cpl Jack Anning's testimony, Smith formulated the battle plan which Yates implemented. The O/C of A Coy was in active control throughout the whole action. Anning, who has a clear memory of the ensuing skirmish, was provided with a Thompson sub-machine gun with which he was instructed to guard Lt Yates who was armed only with a pistol.

About 800 yards out while travelling in open formation, the raiding party was fired upon by several rifles and two machine guns about 150 yards apart and in a line directly in front of the patrol. In dire peril in the open, exposed position they found themselves in and surprised by the strength of the opposition, the platoon went to ground. Having kept the enemy's head down by rapid fire and snap shooting, Robinson took Cpl Curr's section to higher ground while Yates took two sections to a partly dug ditch at right angles to the enemy position. Intending to enfilade the Germans from both flanks, the party continued to fire and snipe until they were nearly out of ammunition. This was a serious situation as there were many more Germans in the ditch than expected.[171]

Smith, noticing no progress after twenty minutes of action, again contacted BHQ, requesting assistance in the form of two Bren Gun Carriers. A messenger arrived from Yates requesting more ammunition and similar assistance soon after. The ammunition plus a 2-inch mortar – a Smith touch – as well as four extra men, were sent onto the field. Bob Scarr recalled that Cpl Ryan, Jim Horton and he formed one carrier crew while Sgt Tom Keys and Jim Christiansen formed the other.[172]

While waiting for those reinforcements, Robinson told Si Cooper, his Bren gunner, to conserve ammunition and only fire if rushed. The carriers under the command of Sgt Tom Keys opened fire, raking the ditch from stem to stern. Much to their relief, Robinson and Sgt 'Long John' Cunningham discerned movement in the ditch: 25 Germans had decided to surrender under a white flag. However, that group, which included several who were wounded and being carried or helped, was then fired upon by their own men – at least seventy in number. About this time Ptes Lutton and Middleton arrived with the sightless 2 inch mortar and proceeded by trial and error to land half a dozen rounds on the enemy position.[173] Robinson recalled that after ten mortar bombs had landed in and around the ditch, the Germans became completely demoralised and stopped firing. Keys reported: 'While the mortars engaged the enemy, the Carriers, under instructions from myself, went to each end of the trench where excellent enfilade fire was obtained. Then moving around to the flanks one Carrier was hit with an A/Tk rifle which was found to be jammed after capture. When the enemy discovered they were trapped, they stood up and surrendered ....'[174]

Refusing to surrender to CSM Robinson, who was a non-commissioned officer, the commander of the large group, who spoke perfect English, asked to be directed to Lt Yates who was 200 yards distant at the western end of the ditch. During the surrender negotiations within the large anti-tank ditch when he found Yates, the German lieutenant colonel sought assurance that his troops would be well treated and the wounded receive medical treatment. He was obviously in charge of his troops, throwing his weight around, barking out orders and expecting instant obedience.

Suddenly a group of prisoners made a commotion, waving the equivalent of a white flag which Ponath equated with cowardice. Drawing his pistol, he fired several shots above their heads. Startled at that sudden burst of fire and taking no chances, Lt Yates shot the German leader above the heart at the close range of one yard. Jack Anning recalled that it was obvious that Ponath had wanted to die and probably knew what his sudden volley would bring.[175]

With the death of the lieutenant colonel, the Germans became completely demoralised and finally gave up. There were no more belligerent stares and curses that Yates's party experienced as they passed some of the reluctant prisoners while moving along the trench, some 200 yards in length. Lt Yates witnessed and recorded the German's last moments as he did not die immediately. As the German hero lay dying, his weeping 2/IC, Captain Bartsch, requested permission from Lt Yates to talk to him. Yates, realising the poignancy of the situation, could only avert his eyes after acceding to the request. When that evidently most revered commander had breathed his last, the loyal officer covered his body with a large swastika vehicle recognition flag, slung him the Nazi salute and performed a snappy about turn. Then, with tears rolling down his cheeks, he formally placed his troops at Yates' disposal.[176]

About this time, Captain Smith entered the field, to take charge of the surrender. Having dropped their arms at Yates's command in the ditch, the Germans were then instructed to assemble at a point in front of a well. Having obtained several buckets, Smith ensured that the prisoners were provided with as much water as they needed. Thereafter the POWs were handed over to the military police who, with a two carrier escort, herded them to the prisoner-of-war camp across the road – the first step on the way to their ultimate destination – Murchison POW Camp in Victoria.[177] Having briefly accompanied Capt Smith to company headquarters, Captain Bartsch complimented him in perfect English on the quality of the company's defensive position.

That action with the leading Company of the 8 Machine-Gun Bn resulted in relatively light German casualties: 3 deaths, 7 badly wounded, 1 slightly wounded and 87 captured.[178] Although it has taken nearly seven decades to make the connection between the rank of the commander and the unit, the highly esteemed dead German officer has definitely been identified as Gustav Ponath – Rommel's champion.

Never had the Australians seen such modern equipment in such quantities – apparently not enough to put up a fight against enfilading carriers and accurate mortar firing. In fact, after A Coy helped themselves to souvenirs, the materiel was removed from the field by the truckload. As victor of the combat, the injured Captain Smith was presented with the enemy 'standard' – Ponath's blood-stained pall. Also his equipment deficiency was rectified by the gift of a luger pistol and binoculars. The only souvenir he could not make use of was a German helmet. Today the flag, luger and helmet can be found as exhibits within the Australian War Memorial in Canberra.

Smith read the early signs witnessed by CSM Robinson as indicators that the German commander aimed to achieve Rommel's goal of reaching Tobruk. After all, the complete *Panzer* and depleted infantry had fulfilled Rommel's objective of reaching the vicinity of the El Adem crossroad. However, Olbrich's *Panzers* had left the dependent infantry in the lurch amid loud argument at the ditch. Yet the still-willing Ponath could see the possibility of assuming charge of the clapped-out tanks himself, overcoming a section of the 2/15 Bn, silencing the nearby RHA and forming a bridgehead with his superbly equipped *Panzergrenadiers.* Certainly, Ponath had demonstrated on the southern perimeter that he was more than capable of establishing and maintaining a bridgehead with a minimum of troops to permit deep enemy penetration by the main body which followed. After all, he took Derna with merely one infantry company, backed by some armoured support.

Greig Smith, who in Condon's opinion, had directed 'a brilliantly successful battle', suspected an impending attack. He commented in his report, after praising Yates and his section for cool determination and courage, that 'the capture of these prisoners saved a probable assault on the 25 pdr battery and this Coy at nightfall'. The establishment of such a foothold in A Coy territory would be the requisite to mount the final attack on Tobruk harbour.[179] In the end, Ponath was frustrated that the damaged tanks could not be restarted, was disillusioned that he had been abandoned by the *Panzer* and watched in disbelief as his elite troops waved the white flag before he had a chance to carry out his nocturnal plan. Ashamed at the loss of face and disillusioned, Ponath basically committed suicide; he would never surrender.

The battle was all but over when B Coy was transported from the King's Cross area to post R30 on the perimeter to bolster the counter-attack. Surprisingly the Germans had abandoned their action in that area, leaving behind a truckload of their dead. Nevertheless, the thwarted Australians had taken one prisoner, a German pilot. In common with most Hun prisoners, he was arrogant and overbearing, boasting that the tables would be turned before the week was out.[180]

Sadly the elation which followed the decisive victory was tempered with tragedy for A Coy. News that the popular Lt Doug Cubitt had been killed in action whilst acting as liaison officer at the 2/17 Bn front circulated among his battalion like brushfire.[181] It was reported that he had been 'knocked over' by machine-gun fire after the battle appeared to be well over.

This accurate account of Ponath's death is far removed from the German version as reproduced by Fitzsimons. This located Ponath in the open, 1500 yards from the ditch in which he was trapped and met his fate. He was leading his troops towards safety beyond the southern perimeter – three miles south of his actual location. After travelling merely twenty yards, it was alleged that he was felled by a 2/17 infantryman, the rest of his company being 'picked off, one by one'.[182] To avoid the ignominy of being trapped and captured in a ditch by a basically-armed platoon , as well as being the first German Army unit to be defeated in World War II, the custodians of that Machine-Gun Battalion's records obviously 'cooked the books'.

That defeat at El Adem Road virtually decimated the 8 Machine-Gun Battalion. Of the 700 troops who comprised that unit three weeks previously, only 300 survived. Those who were killed in action totalled 150 while 250, mainly being wounded, were taken prisoner.[183] Conversely, the 2/15 came through the battle without a casualty at El Adem Road. 'Beginners' luck' commented Cobb, typical of his modesty.

Major Cragg, CO of the 2/15 Bn focused on his own apparent obsession with communication in his summation of his battalion's battle experience. He was pleased that information came through steadily, allowing him to maintain contact with the situation. However, he was severely critical of the Company commanders who moved too much among their troops, thinking erroneously that they would act as a steadying influence. He stressed that interaction was unnecessary and inconvenient as the CO had to waste valuable time whilst he tried to locate some of his leaders. Predictably, special praise was heaped upon the signallers who, under adverse conditions, maintained lines of communication throughout the battalion and even after the passing tanks inadvertently cut the connections. It was left to Brigadier Murray, commander of the 20th Bde to praise the troops of the 2/15 Bn. He congratulated the garrison of Tobruk and his brigade in particular for 'their determined resistance which led to the enemy's defeat.'[184]

Lavarack appeared more generous to his warriors. As Commander of the Western Desert Force, he promulgated a special order of the day which was received 'In The Field' on the evening of Monday 14th April 1941. A Coy's triumph was cryptically alluded to:

> I wish to congratulate all ranks of the garrison of Tobruk Fortress on the stern and determined resistance offered to the enemy's attacks with tanks, infantry and aircraft today.
>
> Refusal of all infantry posts to give up their grounds, a prompt counter attack by reserves of the 20th Bde, skilful shooting by our artillery and Anti Tank guns combined with a rapid counterstroke by our Tanks stopped the enemy's advance and drove him from the perimeter in disorder. At the same time the RAF and our AA defences dealt severely with the enemy in the air.
>
> Stern determination, prompt action and close cooperation by all arms ensured the enemy's defeat and we can now feel more certain than ever of our ability to hold Tobruk in the face of any attacks the enemy can stage.
>
> Everyone can feel justly proud of the way the enemy has been dealt with.
>
> Well done TOBRUK.[185]

In the copy he made in the field, Smith underlined the third line and proudly printed beside it in parenthesis ('Our Coy').[187] Considering that the 2/15 Battalion's action had been singled out by Lavarack as a significant factor in the German defeat, it is indeed a travesty – even sloppy history – that the Bn has been virtually neglected for so long in the many accounts of the Tobruk siege.

When Major Greig Smith died in September 1987, ground-breaking historical research on the nature of the German element of the El Adem conflict was still over two decades away. In delivering his eulogy, Bob Cowie, then president of the 2/15 Bn Remembrance Club, recalled that the Easter Battle was the occasion 'when Greig took a spoke out of the German wheel, inflicting heavy casualties on them and taking a batch of prisoners'.[*]

This was certainly how history would eventually record that conflict, but subsequent research has also shown that it was sweet revenge for the 2/15 Battalion. Such investigation indicated that Lt Col Ponath was commanding a battle-hardened infantry company at the time of his defeat – almost certainly the same body of men who captured Lt Col Marlan, HQ Coy and 100 men at Derna, a matter of days before the Easter Battle. In terms of Aboriginal culture, the death of that German officer and the demise of his formerly invincible battalion constituted a typical example of "payback".

* *Caveant Hostes,* December 1987

chapter 6

THE POST MORTEMS

The final casualty count revealed that the Germans and Italians lost 150 men killed in action. Around 500 were wounded and 250 – many weeping in shame – were incarcerated in the POW cage at King's Cross. In addition 17 of 38 tanks were destroyed and many more severely damaged. From the Australian side, 26 men were killed and 64 wounded, while 2 cruisers and 3 artillery pieces were knocked out.[187] Rationalising the loss of so many from the Axis camp, Rommel advised a surviving officer from the near-annihilated 8 Machine-Gun Bn: 'You mustn't let it get you down. It's the soldier's lot. Sacrifices have to be made'.[188] That soldier would have received little solace from his commander's offhand remarks: his battalion had been reduced from 1400 on arrival in Libya to merely 300.[189]

Yet Rommel was furious and looking for scapegoats. For the slaughter of Ponath and much of his battalion, he placed the blame firmly on the heads of Lieut-Col Olbrich and Maj-Gen Streich. In the case of the former, Rommel fumed that the tanks had left the infantry in the lurch, while the latter never even entered the field of battle, the 5th Light Div being pinned down outside the perimeter by heavy fire. Olbrich and Streich were immediately removed from their commands or were 'put on a camel ride back to Germany', as those in the *Afrika Korps* were wont to say in such situations. Even brave Ponath, whom Rommel eventually accepted to be dead, came in for severe criticism: he wasted too much time filling in the anti-tank ditch at the bridgehead.[190]

In 1986 Miller summarised in his text book for US military officers the factors he considered to have led to Rommel's defeat and Morshead's decisive victory. While he agreed with Rommel's severe criticism of Olbrich's actions and the tardiness of Ponath's engineers, he repeated the long-accepted but incorrect German version of the demise of Ponath and his *Panzergrenadiers* which for nigh on seventy years has been a red herring to the actual situation. Miller also indicated the vital importance of A Coy's action south of King's Cross:

> The clearly recognisable turning point of the battle was when the 5th Panzer regimental commander Colonel Olbrich ordered his forces to withdraw. A mile and one-half inside the Australian perimeter, having reached a slight rise across their front, the Panzers suddenly faced a line of British 25-pounders, anti-tank guns and tanks on their flanks. The British fire was devastating, and seventeen Panzers were destroyed. As soon as the lead Panzer battalion turned to avoid the British fire, it ran into the trailing Panzer battalion. With this reverse in direction came confusion and an immediate shift of momentum to the defenders. This key event was further magnified by the actions of the German 8 Machine-Gun Battalion. Lieutenant Colonel Ponath, the battalion commander, had tried unsuccessfully to prevent Colonel Olbrich from withdrawing. Without tank support, the 8 Machine-Gun Battalion's men were lying on the ground with no cover, under heavy fire, and their ammunition was running short. Colonel Ponath decided to pull the battalion back, and as they made the first rush to withdraw, he was killed, a bullet through his heart. The next senior officer ordered the men to cease fire, and many then surrendered. With this event, the Australian infantry was able to restore the perimeter, except for minor pockets of German resistance ... also the failure of the German engineers to lead the attack columns directly to the perimeter opening, causing a delay in the attack time and the effects of preparatory fires .... Alerted to the imminence of an attack ... General Morshead concentrated his artillery, antitank guns, tanks and infantry reserves to meet the German assault.[191]

In his defence Olbrich listed the mitigating factors which arose from Rommel's arrogance, supreme confidence and poor preparation which Miller viewed as dooming the attack from the start:

- The information distributed before the action emphasised that the Australians were about to withdraw.
- The Australian morale was low and their artillery was weak.
- The infantry would retreat when confronted.
- His regiment had no idea of the well-designed and executed defences of Tobruk.
- They had not the slightest inkling of even one battery position or the large number of anti-tank guns and heavy tanks.

In sum, Olbrich considered that the vastly superior enemy, the frightful loss of Panzers and the lack of any supporting weapons caused his regiment to fail.

The German survivors of the 'Hell of Tobruk' focused upon the qualities of the Australian soldier. One captured doctor who had served throughout the campaigns in Europe remarked to his captors: 'I cannot understand you Australians. In Poland, France and Belgium once the tanks got through the soldiers took it for granted they were beaten, but you act like demons. The tanks break through and your infantry still keep fighting'.[192]

From Major Ballerstedt's intercepted report on the operations in Africa dated 7 June 1941, the translation of 'Infantry Positional Warfare in the Desert' was widely circulated among the besieged. From his experience in France and Libya, he considered the Australians to be 'extraordinary tough fighters', unquestionably superior to the German soldier, especially in the use of ground camouflage and weapons. Possessing the gift of observation and drawing correct conclusions from that process, they were also adept at using every means to take the Germans by surprise. Focusing on the outstanding results of snipers, he noted: 'They shoot at anything they recognise. Several NCOs of the Battalion have been shot in the head with the first shot while making observations in the front line. Protruding sights in gun directors have been shot off, observation slits and loopholes have been fired on, and hit as soon as they were seen to be in use (ie. when the light background became dark). For this reason loopholes must be kept plugged with a wooden plug, then taken out for use, so that they always show dark'.[193]

The Australian snipers were far from being sociopathic killers, Bob Scarr being a shining example of their type. He was both compassionate to his mates and towards the enemy. He felt remorse for each 'poor bugger' he had to take out, but *c'est la guerre*. Poignantly, after the Ponath mop-up, Bob was seen helping a limping wounded German towards the designated assembly point for the prisoners – a well in front of A Coy's line. The gratitude of the new POW for such a display of humanity was evident in the fact that he had slung Bob's .303 with fixed bayonet over his own shoulder. The German had realised that those arms, continually slipping from Scarr's shoulder, got in the way of their progress.[194] Greig Smith shared that care which probably permeated the whole of the 2/15. One of his first actions when the exhausted, half-starved Germans arrived at his HQ was to ensure that they were all provided with water. Then it was off to the POW cage near the road junction.[195]

As the penultimate point in his final assessment of the German failure at Tobruk, Miller concluded that the battle was a set piece for light infantry supported by artillery, armour and anti-tank weapons in the defence against a heavier armed force. When all was said and done, Rommel had been denied a critical objective associated with the failure of his *blitzkrieg* tactics. 'Psychologically, it was a shocking blow to German morale, cohesion and momentum. For the British and their allies, it provided a long-needed boost in morale'.[196]

In inflicting that blow, the 2/15 Bn played a much larger role than has previously been attributed. Rommel considered taking out the defences at the El Adem crossroads as the most important goal of his Easter Monday campaign,[197] and it was there he was finally defeated. His full-strength Panzer and depleted infantry forces achieved the important goal of reaching the King's Cross precinct, but were thwarted by the British artillery and the Queensland-raised battalion in achieving their next goal – the capture of Tobruk. Hence the 2/15 Bn's long-neglected deeds on 14 April 1941 should hereafter take their rightful place as integral to the Tobruk corpus. Further, the widespread ignorance of the incidents attendant to the death of Lt-Col Ponath should be rectified. The new revelations speak of a battalion worthy of a place beside the brave 2/13 and 2/17.

In 1944, Wilmot encapsulated the significance of the Australian/British victory at Tobruk:

> To-day when the myth of German invincibility has been finally dispelled on the battlefields of Russia and North we may be inclined to forget that in April 1941 the Germans were still unchecked on the land. The German forces that Rommel brought against Tobruk came fresh from triumphs that had already carried the swastika from Poland to the Pyrenees, from Norway to North Africa. Until then the German blitzkrieg tactics had never been countered. No force or fortress had withstood the Nazi assault. During the first eighteen months of the war the Allied armies suffered one defeat after another. Then came this siege of Tobruk, and during the next eight months when the German armies in the Balkans and Russia were still carrying all before them, Tobruk alone held out unconquered.[198]

SAVING THE DAY

Despite the determined opposition mounted by the Australians on the southern perimeter, Ponath did establish a bridgehead between two posts of the 2/13. Thereafter thirty-eight tanks with a depleted infantry unit bore down on the El Adem crossroads area. Rommel had achieved his first objective: he had broken through Australian defences and his forces were purposefully advancing on Tobruk. It appeared at that juncture that only the infantry of 2/15 Bn and the Royal Horse Artillery stood in their way. Given the fact that these elements finally repulsed Rommel's force in that area, the 2/15's consequent protective and attacking actions at that critical juncture – the unrivalled bravery of the British gunners apart – could hardly be envisaged as unworthy of historical comment.

In the final count, Tobruk was saved in the vicinity of El Adem Road. While the valiant RHA accounted for the *Panzer,* it became the lot of a rough and tough infantry company from Western Queensland, under the command of a severely injured former bank clerk from the Brisbane suburb of Ashgrove, to clash with – and defeat – the formerly unbeaten, well-equipped Machine-Gun Bn led by a highly decorated German hero.

While the siege has not been entirely forgotten in contemporary Australia, the vital role of the 2/15 Bn has never really been acknowledged. As the 70th anniversary of one of Australia's greatest battlefield triumphs should be remembered in 2011, it is an apt occasion for the significant contributions of the forgotten 2/15 Bn to be belatedly recognised and thereafter enshrined alongside the well-documented, brave actions of its southern comrades-at-arms.

Lt-Col Robert Marlan, CO 2/15 Bn, 1940
2/15 Bn AIF Remembrance Club collection

Capt Greig Smith with the mortar platoon, Darwin 1940
AG Smith collection

Carrier Parade, Darwin 1940
2/15 Bn AIF Remembrance Club collection

Officers of the 2/15 Bn, Darwin 1940

AG Smith collection

2/15 Bn marching in Brisbane, December 1940
2/15 Bn AIF Remembrance Club collection

Queen Mary leaving Sydney with 2/15 Bn, December 1940
AG Smith collection

Sgt John 'Bomber' Neal supervising lifeboat drill on the Great Bitter Lake 1941
John Neal, Townsville

Pre-war Tobruk
2/15 Bn AIF Remembrance Club collection

Maj-Gen Sir Leslie Morshead 1941
AWM, Canberra

Lt General Erwin Rommel
Desmond Young, Rommel, *1950*

Lt-Col Gustav Ponath, CO, 8 Machine-Gun Bn
Axis History Forum

Victorious Lt-Col Gustav Ponath and 8 Machine-Gun Battalion on parade: France 1940

Axis History Forum

AE Battery, 1RHA, 13 April 1941 – KIA
AG Smith collection

RHA 25-pounders in action
AWM, Canberra

Lt Tom Keys, carrier commander at right, with Pte Bob Scarr, crew member and sniper

Greg Snow collection

Anti-tank ditch, Red Line, Tobruk
AWM, Canberra

Capt Greig Smith, Palestine 1941
AG Smith collection

Lt Ron Yates, 1941
William Yates, Toowoomba

Lt. Kevin Robinson
Lindsay Harris collection

Capt Greig Smith at Kantara Hospital after the battle, 1941
AG Smith collection

PART II:

RECORDS OF THE 2/15 BATTALION AROUND EASTER 1941

chapter 7

FROM BRISBANE TO TOBRUK

THE BATTALION IN TRANSIT

CSM Don Parker, 'Infantry Battalion', *CH*, c. 1976, pp.1-12

Early in April 1940 the Commonwealth Government gave permission to form the 7th Australian Division AIF. The Command of the New Division passed to Major General JD Laverack [sic]. The 20th Brigade, of which the 2/15 Bn was a member Battalion, was entrusted to Brigadier JJ Murray.

Major RF Marlon [sic], Brigade Major 11th Infantry Brigade of North Queensland himself a Staff Officer of the Australian Military Forces, was given command of the 2/15 Battalion and was gazetted a Lieutenant Colonel. Lt-Col Marlan visited the units in Queensland to select his Officers and requested units to supply him with suitable NCOs.

By mid June, the Battalion was almost complete in personnel, including men from all parts of the State of Queensland, Papua and New Guinea. Everyone was subjected to all kinds of medical injections and vaccination.

Issue of military clothing and equipment proceeded and squads of men and newly formed platoons drilled in the camp area. Great attention was given to infantry drill, rifle exercises, bayonet training and finally a trip to Enoggera Rifle Range for rifle shooting practice.

Rumour, that deadly and harmful process, had it that the Battalion was off to a place unknown.

On 1st July 1940, 2/15 Battalion embarked at Pinkenba Wharf for Darwin, NT, on board SS "Zealandia". The trip was very smooth process and gave time for the vaccinated to get over their painful sore arms. On board, platoons were lectured by their Officers, as far as facilities on the boat allowed.

Disembarking at Darwin, the Battalion went to Vesteys old meat works for accommodation, and later Companies were allotted other areas. Every day the CO held a parade of Platoons in Company order, and it became evident that the Battalion was taking shape. Being away from Brisbane, the troops were able to settle down away from their relatives and friends.

Sporting facilities were available and intercompany sport thrived. After morning parades, the Companies got on with digging and setting up defences of Darwin and also built a road under the supervision of the 2 I/c Major C[harles] Barton, himself an engineer. Several parades were held in Darwin when the Battalion in Platoon Order, marched past the Northern Australian Commandant, Brigadier Clive Steele.

A few years before the War, a unit "The Darwin Mobile Force" was raised and this group, a picked force and highly trained by this time, made it their business to attack members of the 2/15 and of course, in return the Battalion members sought out and also attacked the members of the Darwin Mobile Force. Fighting of a type took place all over Darwin, any time. The writer remembers such a stoush, when a Sergeant sang "God Save the King", hoping that the combatants would stay their fisticuffs, and stand to attention while such a worthy tune was sung, but the fight still went on – the roving patrol stopped the fight.

During their stay in Darwin, a special sports day was held by the locals on Labour Day 29th July 1940 at Knuckey's Lagoon, and during the day the most important battle up to this kind by the Battalion, took place, it was a free for all affair, and is still referred to.

Early in August, the battalion Routine Order introduced us to the first Colour Patch for the Battalion, this was domed shaped, purple over a red patch, as soon as the colours became known, Captain Andy Skinner, our QM, an old 15th Battalion member of the first World War, let out a howl, taken up by the Angels Club (15th Battalion World War Veterans Club) in Brisbane for its removal and replacement with the original battalion Colours.

After a few weeks in Darwin and Battalion and Platoon drill, A Coy moved to the 8 Mile where extra Platoon training took place and a making of a Defence Road under control of Major Barton was commenced. This work was taken up as a challenge between Platoons and the road started to take shape. B Coy remained at Vesteys and was employed in digging trenches and posts and wiring same in the fanny Bay area.

C Coy used to clean up Vesteys, spent a month on guard duties and digging defence lines at 11 Mile Station, Cemetery Plains and after A & B Coys returned to Brisbane, the Coy spent another month at the 8 Mile and continued the road making started by A Coy and also constructing defence positions at Lee Point, with a final return to Vesteys. A local strike by Darwin workers led to some waterside work being done by the Coy.

D Coy were quartered in Vesteys Meatworks, 2nd floor, and carried out normal training up to Company and Platoon exercises plus guard, piquet and other battalion duties. On the return of A&B Coys to Brisbane, D Coy moved over to the 11 mile to do guard duties at the Wireless Station. After about a month the Coy returned to Vesteys and continued on the cutting of the road to Casuarina Beach and some defence work on the beach front. The work continued until the Company returned to Brisbane in the second voyage of the "Zealandia".

The other battalions of the Brigade, the 2/13 and 2/17 Battalions were preparing to sail to the Middle East.

At first, the proposal was to transfer 2/15 to an 8th Division Brigade, and let a Brisbane Battalion already formed for the next Division to sail in our stead. Evidently, there was some bucking about the transfer, and it was arranged that the 2/25 Battalion would relieve the 2/15 in Darwin. The 2/15 left Darwin to return to Brisbane for final arrangements to proceed overseas.

The return to Brisbane was undertaken in two moves. The first commanded by Major C Barton, was A, B and part of C Company with odds and sods (the sods being the naughty boys of Darwin, being sent out for discharge by Major Barton on our arrival in Brisbane).

After we arrived in Brisbane, the first group were stationed at Grovely until the return of the 2nd group, under the command of Lt-Col Marlan. The Battalion was joined by the first reinforcement Group as well as being brought up to strength on moving to Redbank.

Training was carried out in earnest, Jack Cable taking B Coy, and George Vincent with D Coy in bayonet, training the men into fit soldiers. John Neal of A Coy, was the Arms drill specialist in that Coy, so much so that later, when taking the detention group behind the front at El Alamein, he had the Poms (British Artillery) standing to attention. C Coy had a platoon of marching singers and they really moved along, 15 Platoon setting the standard. Lt Bode of A Coy had his platoon doing all kinds of arms drill while on the march. At this stage and with this type of training, the Battalion was getting there.

Practice in entraining, with full kit became a daily must. The I Section had established a train outlined in mother earth in the camp area, with the type of carriages the Railways were to supply.

On November 11 1940, on the anniversary of the 1918 Armistice, a Special guard of Honour, commanded by Lt Ted Luther of B Coy, and a drill squad prepared by Sgt J Neal of A Coy, attended a service at the Crypt of Anzac Square with the Angels Club (men of the 15th Battalion 1st World War). At a later date another guard of honour was prepared by Sgt Neal for the Divisional Commander Major Gen Lavarack. The general made a few caustic remarks about the young officers Lt-Col Marlan had selected and the CO had to arrange for a few older officers to take their place in the Battalion. I don't think the General would have been so critical had he seen the young devils leading platoons on special patrols on the many fronts the Battalion was given to fight on. Probably it is not fair to state that a few of the older officers brought in at the time did not measure up to Battalion standard.

Into Redbank camp, a young officer brought a Bren Gun, the new unknown weapon in Australian hands. He stood the box on the floor, showed how to assemble it. (But being of Gold set with Diamonds and rubies – no one would dare touch it). And so the introduction of the few to the ordinary infantry weapon was made, and later remade in Palestine when instructors from the 2/15 put in an appearance with this weapon.

Another colour patch, more in keeping with the battalion tradition, was issued, a large diamond patch in grey with the original 15th Battalion in miniature superimposed thereon. At last we were the 15th Battalion going to war. The large grey patch in diamond form being 7th Division distinctive colour form.

A few final parades were called and on one such, the 15th Battalion Angels presented the Band with a sash showing on it the 1st 15th battalion honours, Sgt Jimmy Seaton was the recipient of the sash. This was later lost in the Benghazi handicap.

A few days before leaving Redbank, the CO selected a number of NCOs from each company to remain behind and proceed to Officer's Training Schools. A number of these sought out the CO and told him they wished to go with the Battalion, this he allowed, while others sought out the CO to fill the vacancies so made.

The Battalion with its first Reinforcements marched out of Redbank on the 25th December 1940, Christmas Day. It marched along the platform at Redbank Station, the train pulled in, but the carriages were in the reverse to the practice carriages in which the battalion had trained on the ground. However, all got aboard, with a minimum of fuss, and perhaps the training on the earth drawn carriages had saved broken windows etc, in the train which otherwise could have occurred.

The train pulled out and we later boarded the interstate train at South Brisbane Interstate platform, on the station were many wives, relatives and friends present for the final goodbyes, and in many cases tears.

The battalion left the South Brisbane Interstate Platform at Approx. 4pm, the men waving to their relatives and friends as the train pulled out to go via Kyogle Railway to Sydney. The troops settled down to enjoy the passing sights as the train moved along. There was no stopping for meals, as the watery stew dished out before we left Redbank was the lot for the day and the next morning. Many had, of course, some eats and drinks at South Brisbane platform with friends while awaiting the train's departure plus Comforts Fund and RSL Gifts of sweets from the Salvation Army.

In one of the coaches occupied by B Coy, was the famous placard "From the old 15th to the new". This placard was carried throughout the Middle East and gave good copy to the Australian Papers from Tobruk. It however disappeared on the "Aquitania" and no one had come forward with this very vital memento to the Old and new Battalion relationship.

The train arrived in Sydney at 1pm and went straight out to the wharf where the men moved to a Ferry for ferrying out to the HMT QX, the famous "Queen Mary", the second largest liner afloat. We could see the large gaping hole in the side of the transport and the ferry made straight for it, the troops off loaded and went into the hole, which swallowed up the Battalion effortlessly.... .

During the 26th and 27th December, other elements of 7th Division and reinforcements for the 6th & 9th Divisions came aboard. Lord [Alexander] and Lady [Zara] Gowrie, the Governor-General and his wife, also came to say farewell to the troops.

The 28th December was a fine day and as we left Sydney at 8am with five other troop ships and an escorting cruiser HMAS Canberra, the moving spectacle put on for the NSW members of the ship's party can only happen once in a lifetime and we of Queensland felt that the farewells were for us also. Small craft appeared near the great Liner and fussed around and as the morning wore on there were hundreds of them with eager enquiring faces upturned to the "Queen Mary", scanning the troops for the last glimpse of relatives. Some of the people on the boats displayed banners with messages painted or printed thereon.

It was indeed a rousing send-off and as the liner drew towards the Heads, there were cheers from the troops and shrieks and whistle blasts from the little boats and we [were] also watched by thousands from the cliffs. The small craft followed until the ocean swell through the Heads told them it would be unwise for them to continue further. Quickly the Troopships reached the Heads and moved out to the open sea. Eyes were focussed towards the receding coastline, until the margin of water hid it from sight altogether. Passing well down near Tasmania, we felt the cold and turned west, reaching Freemantle WA and stood out in the Roadstead and of course there was no leave.

On the 16th about noon, we left Colombo with 15 ships in the convoy and soon passed into the Red Sea, boat drill was had, and after a few days we were informed that if the siren went off again it would be the real thing and the men were to act accordingly.

The Band made frequent "blows" on the decks, if it had also played on the "QM" most did not know. The Bandmaster, Norm Henstridge, was congratulated by the Dutch Master of the vessel after a "blow" which included the Dutch National Anthem.

Arriving at Port Suez, we moved into the Suez Canal on 29 January. The weather had changed, it now being very cold, the scenery along the bank was beautiful at the entrance, but later the desert extended on both sides and we made anchor in the Great Bitter Lake – enemy planes welcomed us by dropping bombs and mines. The mines in the Canal to catch the shipping. The ship remained in the lake for 3 days while the mines were being cleared up by planes with great magnetic circles on them, which had something to do with exploding the mines.

Leaving the Great Bitter Lakes we arrived at Ismalia at 9 am on February 3rd, left Ismalia at 6 am on the 4th and arrived at El Kantara at 8 am. Disembarked and entrained in some closed and some open wagons and with a clang and noise, spent a day in a "nightmare" trip until we reached Kilo 89 Gaza Ridge at 8 pm. We were shown into our area by 2/13 Battalion, a sister unit in the Brigade.

Training and route marching began immediately and specialist instructors from 2/13 and 2/17 Battalions took weapon training classes with the Bren Gun, 2" Mortar and the anti-tank rifle.

The Camp became a hive of activity, the movement in the Western Desert gave rise to the thought that we would be too late getting there and there was much hard work preparing for the day we too would be on the move to the Western Desert before fighting etc was over. Troops were marched along the old Turkish defences, which for a long time withstood the battles for Gaza in 1917 and as we also marched along the old Turkish trenches where the Australian Light Horse in the First World War had played a big part in the capture of the ridge from the Turks, we were surprised how well they had stood up to the rigors of time. Marches to and from the well made beach at Gaza, for swimming was a must.

A visit by the Battalion to the rifle range near Jaffa in buses where the drivers tried to outdo each other in speed and turn over the buses – no buses turned over thanks to providence. While in Gaza we were visited by Brigadier J Murray DSO, MC who inspected the Battalion and gave praise at what he saw. We were also visited by the Prime Minister Mr Menzies.

Having settled down, leave for one or two days to visit Gaza, Tel Aviv and Jerusalem was given and much sought after. There was a great cinema in the area which had a change of programme twice a week and a canteen and recreation hut.

Time for movement was coming closer, the CO ordered certain older personnel to be transferred to the Divisional Guard battalion (the Old and Bold) causing a lot of heartburn as the battalion broke up and then there were those to be left behind as a training unit for reinforcements and those returning from hospital. The AIT Battalion was at Murghazi, near Gaza. On the 28th February the battalion left Kilo 89 at 11 pm and marched to Gaza, entrained and set out for Kantara.

At El Kantara on the east bank of the canal, was set up a NAAFI which served hot meals to the Battalion, whether coming or going across the canal. The Battalion crossed the canal by punt and entrained for Mersa Matruh – the crossing of the Nile Delta showed land of extreme fertility, which later merged into arid desert. At ... troops of the 6th Division made available oranges, cake and tobacco. The Desert journey continued and we arrived at Mersa Matruh in the morning at the end of the railway line in bitter wind and rain. We were then lifted to a much bombed and deserted Barracks – a wet miserable and tired unit. The barracks buildings were in a filthy condition and shattered walls bore evidence of severe bombing to which the place was subjected. The next morning was bleak and cold but without rain. We received a rum ration.

The town nestled on a flat between the harbour and the low lying hills to the south. The harbour was small and difficult to enter. The town had been well laid out in squares with tree lined bituminized roads – most of the town was in ruins. The Lido Hotel and the old Mosque seemed unharmed in amongst such bitter desolation. Perimeter defences of mine fields and barb wire surrounded the town.

On 4th March we left Mersa Mathruh by truck and travelled across the desert over many bad roads until Sidi Barani was reached, the scene of earlier action by British Troops, enemy equipment scattered on all sides; Allied bombing and shelling was very much in evidence. The halt for the night was at Bug Bug [or Buq Buq] which had been developed into a main watering point for convoys and again at Bug Bug, enemy equipment lay everywhere.

The next day an early start was made on a cold desert morning. The tarmac ended in the village of Sollum, overhead was the escarpment 600 feet high. There were two ways of reaching the escarpment – 1. a steep climb of up to three miles to Sollum Fort or 2. about a mile inland from lower Sollum up to Halfaya (Hellfire) Pass. Sollum also showed evidence of previous action.

Leaving Egypt behind, the roads were very good. On all sides were masses of Italian equipment, vehicles, field guns, rifles and planes were passed or being looked over by the Salvage Corps. The route ran through the outer defences of Bardia but our view was a distant one. The road crossed the Bardia perimeter, guarded by a tank trap 10 feet wide, beyond was a barbed wire fence of many thicknesses.

In mid afternoon the convoy passed through the outer perimeter of Tobruk and proceeded to a staging area among the wreckage of Italian planes, guns and tanks. So this is Tobruk – we were to remember it well at a later date.

TOBRUK, where the Italian Defences were cracked so easily, and where one of its finest Navalcraft was sunk, was the only good harbour between Alexandria (Egypt) and Benghazi, and it had been built at an enormous cost. In there were a few good springs of fairly pure water and the only good water plant between Derna and Bug Bug.

During the afternoon there was an air raid warning and next a sand storm (Khasmin) and the dust blotted out everything and brought all movement to a standstill. Orders were received for the Battalion to move to Mersa Matruh and relieve elements of the 6th Division entrenched there.

Before leaving Tobruk, many members of the Battalion explored the area and played with the little "Red Devils", grenades of which the Italians left behind literally millions, tasted of the wines, rum and smoked cherottes.

An early start was made on the 6th March and we followed the 2/13 along the Derna Road, much better going than before, passing through Acroma and then Gazala.

About 11am we saw 5 Henkel planes attack the 2/13 Bn convoy ahead causing casualties. Our trucks screamed to a halt in the wake of 2/13 Bn and we received a good lesson from their experience, to keep a good look out and be ready. When the convoy moved on, we drove down the steep pass into the white washed village of Derna with its magnificent shrubs and flowering vines. Looked a nice little place, passing out of the town we camped to the west of it for the night and the first thing in the morning set out for Barce. This country was more fertile and the settlement scheme of Mussolini's was in real evidence, colonial houses and farmsteads and newly ploughed ground were indeed a sight, after the long desert trek. Italian families were seen in the area.

We did not enter Barce, but passed to the left where there was a big P.O.W. camp on our right, with a large number of prisoners within. Our next stop was Tocra (while not being of Biblical importance, Tocra and Cyrene are of great historical importance). At Tocra were great stores of shells and arms, evidently years of preparations. At night we heard the rumble of bombs falling on Benghazi.

On the morning of the 8th we left Tocra and bypassed Benghazi and passed along a beautiful avenue of Australian gums and a native village and again passed out into the desert. Later, a few members of the Battalion did go into Benghazi, but reports indicated that it had collapsed and was no longer was city, but a ruin.

The 2/13 Battalion pulled off at Beda Fomm and we passed by and through the wreckage, scattered in wild confusion, of what had been once an Italian Armoured Division. We moved on and camped at Agedabia. On the following morning, 10th March, we moved forward to Mersa Brega, occupied by elements of 2/5 and 2/7 Battalions of the 6th Division. B, C and Don Coys occupied the marshes on the left flank and the village of Mersa Brega on the right flank. A Coy took up positions on Cemetery Hill, 11th March forward of the general line of defence. To the rear of our Battalion the 2/17 Battalion occupied defence positions.

The troops settled in, a little digging, rifle shooting at empty tins under instruction, and of course we came in contact with the turd beetle, which I think most of us were pleased to escape from, even under as worrying circumstances.

A few forward patrols were made towards El Agheila – (1) by Lieut Bode from A Coy, who went so far as to hear the enemy talking (2) by Lieut AL MacDonald with a Sergeant and 8 men and an escort of two armoured cars, they travelled about 45 miles without contact, but saw trails left by reconnoitring tanks. (3) by Sgt Col Logan of B Coy out into the desert east then west but when out some distance was informed by an Officer in a Scout car of the presence of German vehicles, and had a long journey back (4) by S/M Don Parker of B Coy who took a patrol forward of B Coy, passed Cemetery Hill for a distance of some 15 miles, a British tank officer warned against continuing the journey by foot and the patrol returned.

On the fronts generally, the sections were visited by Wogs [Italians] selling eggs, although orders had been issued to keep these people out of the defences, the men did not see any danger, until S/M Parker had one arrested and sent back to BHQ. This man was an Italian officer doing the egg stuff like the other Wogs. It would appear that the men only act when something out of the book occurs.

From the beginning of our occupying of the area, the German manned aircraft strafed the troops, the roads and all movable things in the area. It is still in the writer's mind that the laughing Hun firing from the tail gun, as he crossed over HQ Coy, was enjoying his job.

In the Battalion were a number of men from North Queensland, proficient in the Italian language, and when the sig attached to the company listened in – in his wireless pack, many of the troops understood the Italian spoken, within a few days a new language was spoken, German not understood by the troops who knew Italian.

No one told us that the German troops were already there, but it was learned from a *North Queensland Register*, received by a soldier from North Queensland, that 100,000 Germans had landed in Tripoli.

On the visit of General Neame to the area, he appeared baffled when told the Germans were in Agheila and wanted to listen in on sig radio.

Now this is the position, did the powers that be know the Germans were there or did they not. Barton Maughan in his book "Tobruk and El Alamein" states the Germans were already in the El Agheila area when the 2/15 Bn took over the front. Members of the 6th Division, from whom we took over, had no more information than what we had.

General Morshead was surprised that the Mersa Brega area had been chosen for defence and that the vital defile, west of Agheila had not been secured, and the troops were not holding El Agheila itself.

One morning, a camel driver tried to drive a herd of camels over the mine field near the marshes. Lieut R[obert] Donnan informed the driver in sign language, the driver then drove off with his camels. It was evident that someone was trying out the mine field, and got their answer.

Our first casualty occurred in the minefield, when Kev Crocker was killed. This had an effect on the troops who thereafter began to give some respect to mines and mine fields.

On 17th March General Morshead requested that 20th Brigade be relieved as the Battalion armament was far from complete. A body of Free French arrived on armed vehicles and were amazed when they learnt that the Germans strafed the area and were in the El Agheila area. They moved out jolly quickly but were to return with the 1st Tower Hamlet Rifles on the night of 22nd March, when we were lifted back to Agedabia and later to a plateau east of Benghazi.

Before leaving Kilo 89 in Palestine, we had on General Blamey's order, become the 9th Division, supposedly temporarily, but of course we were not notified. I think we were in Tobruk for some time before Brig. Murray ordered a diamond shape 7th Division to be changed to the round shape of the 9th Division. At this stage of our move back, it was not expected that the enemy would advance beyond Strafed.

On 23rd March, Rommel ordered the attack to proceed and he took El Agheila. The 20th Brigade were told now to make ready in defence of the escarpment east of Benghazi and stop the enemy coming from the plain. Two roads led to the plain, one from Er Regima and one from near Tocra. The 20th Brigade had to defend the road and railway at Er Regima Pass. The Er Regima Pass to be defended by the 2/13 Battalion and the 2/15 was to take up defensive positions near El Abair. On the 27th March the Battalion walked from the vicinity of Er Regima to El Abair about 8 miles, there were large herds of sheep in the area. At this stage, the Battalion was some 100 miles from Mersa Brega, now held by the Armoured Division and relief forces. At El Abair the battalion dug defensive positions and did much patrolling down the railway towards Benghazi. ....

Up to this stage the withdrawal of the Battalion and in fact the 20th Brigade was fixed as part of a defence system. But [following] the resumption of the German Forces push past Mersa Brega and Agadabia, a general withdrawal was authorised.

The Benghazi Handicap was started

The Battalion was ordered to move to the southern pass, due east of Barce, we moved in a motley lot of trucks, on Italian prime movers – pulled by an Italian long truck with no engine up the pass. On the way we saw prisoners from the POW camp making off in all directions, while the guarding Platoon of another Battalion was walking up the pass. Having reached the top of the pass, the CO [Marlan] set about defences. B Coy at first straddled the main road. ..... B Coy moved with C Coy further around the escarpment and A Coy was left in defence of the road through, while D Coy manned the left side of the pass.

Late in the afternoon of the second day, I was sent over to see the Adjutant, Captain N[eal] Currie, and the RSM Arthur Cotman, both thought the situation bad. At the time I did not feel so, we were trained to fight and saw no reason why we could not do a good job, at least as good as the 2/13 at Er Regima. There I received orders for the movement of the Company later in the evening, which I related to the Coy Commander, Captain Bruce Strange, on returning to the Company. ....

A and Don Coys received orders to retire, A Coy first, followed by Don Coy an hour later. Instruction to Captain Peek of Don Coy if they were cut off by enemy to make for the ocean and signal for sea help. Captain Peek advises that A Coy had not gone long, when the advance guard of Germans arrived and he states they could see all the Iti prisoners in the POW Compound being set free.

The Company with a 2 lb Breda gun set up in the rocks, looking down the pass, this was sighted and set by looking down the barrel. As the leading German vehicle came up the pass, the Coy let go with the Breda, which hit the vehicle head on. Germans scattered in all directions to take cover, but the Brens and rifles of the Company collected the lot.

The Company moved out along the coast road to Derna where it stopped and breakfasted before moving along to Gazala and then to Acroma. The orders to the battalion were to proceed to Giovanni Berta and turn right along the Derna Road to Martuba. The Companies were picked up and moved along the main road, on each side of the road were troops and guns, the troops asleep and not knowing that the last of the infantry were moving out. Some of the Battalion Headquarters and HQ Coy got to the turn off where they were told by a Brigadier that the direct Desert Road had been cut by the enemy. I had a consultation with the Company commander and he said if you can lead us through Derna, do so. One of the Company trucks with Lieut R Donnan and one section of B Coy continued along the Desert Road and of course became prisoners. The rest of the Companies followed us through Derna. At the top of the pass, the Germans were causing havoc on the aerodrome, but moved off as the Companies appeared, the writer shot one of the Germans who talked too much. Moving down the main road, we breakfasted. We then moved down and crossed through a line of Australian soldiers spread out seemingly for miles near Timini, where we were directed to take up a position at Ain El Gazala, the Liaison Officer from brigade met us and told Company Commanders where we were to take up defensive positions. Major Alec Ralston of A Coy took over temporary command of the battalion.

All through the afternoon, trucks arrived, head to tail, until late in the afternoon when a slowing down of truck arrivals showed most were clear, much dust each side of the road heralding the arrival of enemy armour.

At Gazala on top of the escarpment were guns, machine guns and armoured cars and the troops of the Battalion felt now for once we were ready to fight with good supporting weapons. Before dark the mass of armament moved off again and we few infantrymen, now without our CO were holding a position below the escarpment in the dark. Before mid-night we climbed the escarpment and in the dark awaited the lorries to take us elsewhere, which was to be in the area called Acroma.

(I don't like to take the recognition of any event from any person, but many members of the battalion are of the opinion that Captain Andy Skinner led the Battalion from Giovanni Berta to Gazala, indeed it was the writer [Don Parker] and it was not well on in the afternoon that Captain Skinner and CSM George Bannister passed through our defences at Gazala).

We were dumped on Acroma and it was not until morning that Officer Lieut GA Gemmel-Smith with Lieut Morrison in tow saw us to our defensive positions. Gemmel-Smith had been with the CO's party on the desert road but had been sent to find the companies.

Lieut Gemmel-Smith writes to me that Maughan's account of the capture is not strictly accurate. He states the rifle Companies had left before BHQ, whereas BHQ led, followed by HQ Coy and then the rifle Companies. Mine was the leading vehicle of the Battalion and which I shared with Tom Tartallan. In giving his orders the CO said that if we ran into trouble I was to guard the Battalion to the coast where we would trust in the Navy. Major Charles Barton was in charge of our group and I recall one of our hourly stops his being quite amused at the thought of guiding the Battalion anywhere in the state of confusion that reigned. It was after BHQ and HQ Coy passes through Giovanni Berta that the rifle companies were diverted to go through Derna.

Lieut Gemmel-Smith further states – "BHQ and HQ Coy stopped near Martuba at first light and had breakfast while waiting for the rifle Companies. A Royal Engineer Officer, who had been doing demolitions, passed through, he told us he understood the Gerry was five miles to our left front, putting him between us and the coast road. The CO sent me with driver Bill Duncan and Osti Ostburg to see if the road was open and he planned to get the convoy moving. It was about 14 miles to the Coast Road which I found open and by the time I got back to the Battalion the group ware safely in the bag and all I could see from the crest of the rise nearby were some burning vehicles.

On the way back I passed two Tommy Three Tonners whose canopies were shot up and from whom I learned that Gerry was not far behind. We then proceeded to Gazala where I joined the rifle Companies."

The 20th Brigade was guarding the open Desert flank to the left of the main Derna road. Talk was rife about the loss of the CO, BHQ and HQ Company personnel. It was learned that the Germans had constructed a POW camp on the Derna Airfield and arrangements for a rescue party were at hand. Lieut Bode was the Battalion officer and Major 'Bluey' Allen from Brigade. Much bad feeling was generated in the Companies, by selection of men who did not want to go with the party as it was expected that any rescue team would run into the enemy's full force, even the O/C Armoured Cars protested against the misuse of four cars at night, but was ordered by general Morshead to carry on.

The team moved out late, but were delayed near Gazala by the demolition of the previous day and were unable to make the Derna Airfield in night hours, so returned to Acroma with its task unfulfilled.

In the morning, just after stand to, Don Coy charged the rear of B Coy. The writer hearing heavy footsteps, moved out and stopped Lieut Tas Davies and WO Dave Scroggins, with pistols drawn, leading Tas's Platoon with fixed bayonets. The Coy moved off and later made a similar move against A Coy and only the presence of mind of A Coy commander [Capt Greig Smith] saved what could have been heavy casualties. ....

On the night of 9/10 April, the Battalion moved into the Tobruk Perimeter. The night was dark and the track to the main road rough and ill defined. The leading truck of the Convoy got off the track and after about half an hour it was found that the whole Convoy was going around in a circle. The main road was later reached and the trucks ground to a snail's pace owing to the large stream of traffic going into Tobruk. Once inside, the Battalion pulled up and it was no time before the weary troops were asleep.

A POW'S LAST DAYS IN LIBYA

Cpl Alex Connor, 'Approved to wear five service chevrons', *CH*, September 1987, pp. 6-10

There was motor transport sufficient for only one Bn out of three in the Brigade, so two walked while the other rode or walked while waiting for the return of the vehicles. Other units started to roll back, a few artillery, anti aircraft, air force, engineers and other strays. There was no co-ordination and complete radio silence reigned.

At Benina a group of us was lucky enough to find water in the cooling tower of the local pumping station. It was fresh but covered in oil. We went in boots and all, the first fresh water for a month and it felt good. Then the Bn was debussed at the foot of Benina pass and up we climbed. Heavy work with a full pack and 180 rounds of ammunition. Some begged lifts. I decided to walk to prove I could do it and made the grade. The view on the way up was magnificent. As we climbed, we witnessed the destruction of dumps at Benghazi. Also inspected an Italian war memorial of those who had fallen in the Senussi campaign. At the top was a low forest of pine. The officers declared there was no water but a few of us decided that they were wrong. We found 13 wells to prove our argument. We also found some food dumps not destroyed including one of cream – it proved to be mosquito cream.

The Bn maintained a defensive position until the balance of the units was clear then walked to the East for some miles. It was hard work as the sloping hills were grassy and our boots slipped continually. By nightfall we had reached a selected site and slept in the open. Snakes were everywhere, even in our blankets and packs. We moved on the next day and then embussed, travelling all night.

Next morning, April 7th the sun rose on a scene of utter confusion. As we rubbed the sleep from our eyes, weary from bouncing around in the lurching truck and with no comfort except our pack as a rest, we could see stretched out before us a huge dusty undulating plain. No grass, no trees, no habitation, simply a mass of dust covered transport of all makes and purposes, fleeing steadily eastward to Tobruk. There was no road, just dusty trails. The vehicles were constantly changing course to circumvent natural obstacles, and no unit formation existed. There was no attempt being made to control movement.

The 2/15 Bn CO "Spike" Marlan, decided it was essential he gather his unit together, so those trucks transporting his men were halted. About one hundred and fifty gathered, mainly Bn HQ personnel, HQ Coy and some B Coy men. Also with the group were several trucks belonging to a Victorian Anti Aircraft unit. These men were using Italian trucks with a light Italian anti aircraft gun (a Breda) mounted on a pedestal on the back tray. The group were ordered to eat and then proceed on to the east. Hardly had the bully beef and biscuits been produced when an alarm was given. Armour had been sighted to the south, covered in a dust cloud as we had been a few moments before hand. The units were told to move when over our heads flew aircraft not from the RAAF. The half dozen planes buzzed our group, gave no signals, flew off over the armoured group, then disappeared east. It was decided the armour was not offensive, probably being a portion of the British 7th Armoured Division. The 2/15 Bn CO decided to halt a few more minutes to collect his unit.

In next to no time the armoured group swung around our force from the south to the east, unlimbered anti tank guns and set the trucks on fire with their shells. With no equipment except rifles a couple of light machine guns (Breda infantry side feed equipment firing a bullet not much larger than a .22) the two anti aircraft guns which were too light a calibre and a 3" mortar which would not fire, it was a hopeless affair. Within a brief time the whole group were captured and forced to drop weapons and march back some miles to a deep wadi.

There we found other miscellaneous groups including Sudanese, British and Australian units all under guard of a German armoured group, part of which had flown in by Junker aircraft using the bitumen road near Derna as an airstrip. No food or water or supplies were handed out. Some of our men were injured but there was little we could do except apply the first aid kit each of us carried. The men were held overnight sleeping on the ground. I was extremely tired having had little sleep over the past week, trying to keep my section on the move and ensuring security etc was fully sustained. The night on the ground provided a respite which was most welcome.

Captured with the group were General O'Connor, and two other very senior British leaders. Eventually the mass of men were instructed to get up, form threes and prepare to march to Derna. The group, being a mixture and lacking the usual leadership of their own NCO's was lethargic. In no time the

German colonel [Ponath], a most dynamic man armed with a sub machine gun, swung into action and left no doubt in any man's mind that he expected us to be ready in about one minute or else he would shoot. This proved a most effective solution. This particular colonel became well known for his drive, courage and personality. Everyone who became a prisoner even later on had some knowledge of the man and all conceded he was a top class man. He was finally reported to have lost both legs at Tobruk. Even his own men ran when he spoke and his motorcyclists and drivers never ceased to move their equipment at top speed.

The weary column moved off in the direction of Derna under escort, stumbled down the pass in the night and marched through the battered streets, finally to what had been the local hospital. There we were held in an open courtyard, still without food or water and many drank from the fountain in the courtyard, only to incur violent stomach ache. Next day the group was moved through the streets to the Italian barracks, built of concrete and sited at the foot of a cliff. There was a centre courtyard, open rooms to the east and west with latrines to the south side. The Italian guards were scared, extremely trigger happy and spent most of the night hurling grenades at the barracks in the hope that we would not break out. The men slept on concrete floors without cover. The water was in short supply, coming in hand drawn carts and ladled out a little each day to each man. Food was that from a British food dump, previously set on fire and consequently the tins were blown from the heat. The contents were unfit for consumption.

However, there was nothing else so we ate and incurred the most violent form of dysentery. The Italian toilet facilities collapsed under the strain and we were forced to dig open trenches in the courtyard for latrines. There was no paper or water or cover material for the night soil. Most men were unable to control their movements and were reduced to desperate straits. A form of green liquid constantly oozed from ones backside. There were no bathing facilities. Men queued constantly to gain access to the trenches and many failed to get there. As one fellow put it, he could bend over and hit a fly at twenty yards without the slightest effort, such was the pressure built up in the stomach system. The days were long with nothing to do. I possessed only boots, sox, shorts, shirt and a jacket. No toilet gear or mess gear, nothing to read. Most of the time was spent talking to others in the immediate area.

Minor level contact was established with an occasional Italian guard by speaking Latin or French.

On April 13th 1941 the Germans came again and loaded the group on to open flat top Italian diesel trucks. To ensure none escaped, each vehicle carried armed guards in the cab and on the back of the vehicle. There was also at least one utility type German truck fitted with twin machine guns and a bucket seat. The seat swung with the guns by a simple foot traverse. The prisoners were packed in so tightly that it was impossible for all to sit. So some stood and waited their turn for a rest. No one was allowed to leave the vehicles despite the virulent form of dysentery that had spread through the group. Food was confined to Italian hard tack biscuits and a little water. The biscuits which we encountered on and off for some months were a revelation. It was impossible to break the biscuit with one's teeth, rather the teeth crumbled. I broke pieces off most of my top teeth thanks to the baker's technique. There was no flavour and as far as the men were concerned, no nourishment either. However, when hungry, men are willing to try anything. Later it was discovered the biscuits could be made more digestible by soaking them overnight in water. Others tried toasting them. Some bashed them with stones and tried to reduce the biscuit material to a flour but the Central Australian blacks probably fared better on nardoo. The only effective use discovered for the biscuits was to carve out the centre and mount treasured photographs in the opening. At least the frame would not shatter.

The convoy of some hundreds of prisoners were driven to Benghazi non-stop except for refuelling vehicles. Passing German convoys expressed their confidence in being in Cairo in a matter of days. The reply from the Australians was you have to take Tobruk first and there you will meet your match. It was interesting to note the utter contempt held by the Germans for their allies, the Italians. Without question the Italian troops were pitiful. We even witnessed a German machine gunner in the utility firing over the heads of the Italian convoy that had stopped to abuse the prisoners. The Italians moved on very smartly with their trucks piled high with beds and mattresses, heading for the front line.

At Benghazi the men were housed in huge concrete buildings, probably motor workshops at one stage. Food and water were still a problem. It seemed a long way back to the previous Easter holidays spent at Burleigh Heads [in Queensland].

After a matter of some days the convoy was placed back in trucks, this time with Italians only as guards. The road led along the coastline past Mersa El Brega with nothing to see except sand. There was no cover against the weather. Sand blew from the west and made our lives a little more unpleasant. Convoy after convoy of German armour kept moving down the road in the opposite direction and our hearts sank at the sight for we knew the Ninth Division had nothing to equal what the Germans possessed. Italian convoys also went by but they were regarded as a source of amusement. When night came, the convoy stopped but no one was allowed out of the trucks. Several men tried but they were fired upon by the trigger happy Italians. It was no joke filling in that night.

The trucks moved on next day virtually non-stop. At nightfall the vehicles pulled into a small seaside village, possibly Syrts or Misurata (I have forgotten which) [the latter]. There we were driven at bayonet point into Italian barracks. It was a frightful place. The latrines were flooded and the men were so ill with dysentery that the place became a shambles. Most were too exhausted after the trip to help themselves. They lay down and slept where they could. As they slept, the Italians came in during the night and stripped them of their valuables and gear. The theft was not discovered until day broke and the men were herded back to the trucks. The tension in the air was most noticeable. The Italian troops responsible were the Bersaglieri (Roosters as the boys called them because of their Black Orpington feathers in their hats).

Next day the countryside improved a little. Dates groves appeared. So did mud dwellings of Arabs and the quaint water system whereby buckets of water were filled out of wells by using a long rope over a pulley and towed by an animal. The poor beast moved backwards and forwards, waiting each time for the bucket to fill or be emptied. The old roads were so scoured out that the men in the convoy could barely see the drays of Arabs as they progressed down their canal-like lanes. At one stage during the day I developed such a longing for fruit that I successfully bartered an Australian collar badge for a lemon, eating its seeds, rind and all. It was delightful. The convoy stopped overnight at another village and then moved on to the railway station at Tripoli.

That proved to be an interesting place. Because some RAF planes bombed the waterfront, most of the native population was at the railway, loaded with colossal bundles of household goods. As each train pulled in, the natives heaved, shoved, climbed and clambered aboard. Some carriages had an outside staircase giving access to wooden seats on the roof. These were rapidly occupied with masses of people and their possessions. Others hung half way in or out of windows. Others clung to the buffers between carriages. The station possessed no platform so control of passengers was non-existent. The prisoners were assigned to open four sided trucks such as coal is moved in. Those with dysentery simply squatted beside the track in full view of the populace and relieved themselves while waiting for an engine. The guards were still Italian and hopeless they were too.

Eventually the train load of prisoners travelled miles to the West, pulling up at a God forsaken place called Sabratha. It was April 21st. In ancient days the town was a Roman centre complete with amphitheatre. The town had no beauty in the eyes of the current visitors. Sand, hovels, some cultivated areas and a holding camp for prisoners. Simply the standard type of Italian barrack surrounded by wire and guards. There was even a high wall with one portion collapsed. Through it could be seen the old Roman structure. Having nothing to do, the mob used to congregate at this point to look at the building. The guards panicked and rebuilt the wall presumably because they thought that we were planning a break.

Food changed a little at Sabratha. At 6.15 am a small container of sweet black coffee was served. At 11 am there was a ladle of unsalted unflavoured macaroni issued plus two small loaves of bread and one lemon. At 5 pm Italian bully beef (horse flesh?) or a small piece of fresh meat was issued. Very occasionally this was supplemented by raw Sicilian wine or a teaspoon of aniseed. On some occasions the men were given a cubic inch of cheese. Sixty cigarettes were issued one day. The bread was foul. It was extremely doughy, grey in colour and smelt sour. Men tried toasting it and drying it but the bread still gave most of us tremendous stomach aches, primarily producing wind. Because the macaroni and bread worsened dysentery, I became a coffee addict for the first time in my life. By skilful manipulation in queues, I found it possible to obtain up to four servings of the strong sweet coffee (about two teacups in volume). On that alone I existed for some weeks. There was one good laugh during the stay at Sabratha. A prisoner complained of constipation. How we longed to have his trouble. Sleeping conditions were better than encountered elsewhere. Each of us had a rush mat upon which to sleep on the concrete floor.

There was nothing to do at the camp except go to Mass (conducted weekly in Italian and Latin). I did that for some form of diversion. I used to go along with Jim McCauly whom I first met at Darwin in 1940. Most of the men, both Australians and other nationalities, virtually would have nothing to do with their officers or senior NCOs. Rank counted for nothing. Units ceased to exist. Men grouped, broke and regrouped according to their needs, mutual interests and fellowship. Flies were bad.

Some time passed by, then word came that half the mob was to be shipped to Italy. A group of some 500 or so was formed on May 3rd and marched back to Sabratha station. There some bright soul started to baa like a sheep, then a dog barked and a voice called out as if a chap was handling sheep in a yard. In no time the mob responded the same way and it was absolutely laughable watching the Italians trying to get the men into the coal trucks again. They simply could not comprehend the reason for the racket nor why we should be laughing. In their eyes, we should have been downhearted. Only they should have been happy as they were being repatriated to Mumma in Italia.

As the train clacked its way back over the desert to Tripoli the guards sang and the Australians told them they would never see home again as the RAF or Navy would sink their vessels in the Med. As we approached the old city of Tripoli, our spirits rose for we could see huge columns of smoke at the waterfront. The RAF had been there the previous night! The train was halted and we waited until dark then back we came, jolting along and singing at the top of our voices. This time the guards were silent. Next night 500 English and Australians were marched out and reached Italy for they did not return.

Eventually another try was made to shift the prisoners to Italy. On the train again (May 12th) and this time no RAF so we reached the waterfront and were escorted to the "Victoria", sleeping on mattresses in the holds. Food was quite good. Red wine, fresh bread rolls and a reasonable hot dish. Even cigarettes though they were pretty foul. The crew never left their life jackets off and kept their boots unlaced. We were given no life jackets. We were allowed up top to attend the latrine and so saw the convoy. It had about four vessels with four times the number armed escort, mainly destroyers. No submarine halted our progress and we entered Napoli harbour at 4 pm on May 14 1941.

chapter 8

THE BATTALION'S PART IN THE EASTER BATTLE

AN ACCOUNT OF A COY'S INVOLVEMENT

CSM Kevin Robinson, *CH*, June 1976, pp. 23-5

Much shelling had been going on, on the afternoon and night, on the perimeter to our immediate front (2/13 & 2/17 Bns). After midnight the noise and shelling intensified and at about 2 am Captain Greig Smith our CO issued instructions for the Company to "stand to". Everyone in the Company "stood to" until daylight, and as dawn broke and visibility cleared about 7-8 am, a detachment of tanks was seen manoeuvring about 1000 yards in front of us behind the 2/17 Battalion defensive area. A Company was dug in around and protecting a troop (4–25 Pounders guns) of the Royal Horse Artillery and when the gunners realised and made sure the tanks were enemy and not ours, they opened fire.

From our observation they hit several tanks and then about 8 or 10 started to advance in line head formation towards us and the guns and firing as they advanced. The gunners hit the 4th tank in line and it stopped, halting the ones behind it, but the leading tanks continued to advance. When they reached a point only 30 yards from our 8 Platoon but immediately in front of a dummy minefield, consisting of aerial bombs and laid by the Ities, they stopped evidently suspecting the mines and bombs were alive. By this time they were slightly behind the line of the 25 pounders who couldn't fire at them at because they couldn't traverse their guns sufficiently around from their dug in positions. By this time several of the gunners on the second, third and fourth guns were casualties from the enemy machine gun fire but number one gun crew was intact. When the leading tank halted it traversed its gun and with its first shot from a stationary position scored a direct hit on Number one gun and killed or wounded the crew. Members of 8 Platoon now started firing down the barrels of the guns on the tanks at about 30 yards range and kept up a constant spatter on the tanks. The three tanks then turned around and headed off back down towards their starting point and joined the others who also retired. The gunners then engaged them again and knocked out 3 or 4 as they were milling around, about 1000 yards away. Evidently the 3 tanks did not realise that they were not being followed by the remainder of the squadron and as soon as they saw they were on their own, they beat a hasty retreat.

As the Machine Gunners from the tanks had now ceased, we got out of our pits and started to observe what was going on in the German tank area. I had a small pair of binoculars (the only one in the Company) and standing on the sandbags around our pits, I saw the German tank crews from the knocked out tanks taking cover in what appeared to be a half dug tank trap. I noticed probably 12 or 15 crew members run for cover as our 25 Pounders were still firing on the area. I reported this to the Company Commander, Capt Greig Smith, and requested permission to take a party or patrol down to the area and try to capture these Germans as Prisoners of War. By this time, the remaining 8 or 10 'going' tanks had headed back to the perimeter, so capture of the men left behind did not seem a very big job, especially as some of them were probably wounded. Captain Smith agreed to my request and sent me to Lieut Yates of 9 Platoon with a message for him to take his platoon to the area.

After a bit of hurried organisation we got underway and covered approx 1000 yards in smart time. When we were about 200 yards from the position I estimated the enemy were, we were suddenly fired on by several rifles and what appeared to be 2 machine guns – about 150 yards apart and on a line directly in front of us. The whole Platoon went to ground as we were in an open position, absolutely no cover, and suddenly surprised by the opposition we had struck. After some rapid fire, snap shooting from all members of 9 Platoon at any movement they could see in their front, we managed to keep the Germans' heads down and the enemy fire slackened off. Lieut Yates and I had a sharp conference and it was decided that I would take one section, Corporal Curr's, and try to take up a position on our right on some slightly higher ground. Lieut Yates would take the other two sections in another partly dug tank ditch at right angles to the enemy's position. Our idea was to try to enfilade the Germans from both flanks as they were in a partly dug tank ditch also. By making 50 yards bursts in groups of three, the section I was with made the slightly higher ground we wanted, then proceeded to again open fire on the enemy position.

At this stage we had not suffered any casualties and all the men in Corporal Curr's section were doing a fine job of keeping the enemy's heads down. After some 10 or 15 minutes of sniping, I suddenly realised that I had only 5 rounds of ammo left. A quick check among the men in the section, revealed almost everyone was down to his last few rounds. I realised that if the Germans got desperate and attacked us, we would be in a pretty desperate position as by this time we realised that there were many more of the enemy there than the few tank men we expected. I told everyone to cease firing, and only fire on plainly exposed targets and I told Bren gunner "Si Cooper" (later killed at Alamein), who said he had half a mag left, to cease firing altogether and only shoot if he was rushed. I then despatched a runner off the Company to acquaint Captain Smith with the situation and asked for some arms and Mortars, if any were available.

I could still hear a good volume of fire coming from Lieut Yates' two sections over on our left, so I knew we had the situation under control on that flank. While Sgt John Cunningham and I were having a good look at the German lines, we noticed several of the enemy nearest to us, moving up and down the ditch. To our utmost surprise and relief one of them stood up and waved a white flag. Then about 12 to 15 stood up in a group under the white flag and moved out towards us. While this was going on Privates Lutton and Middleton from 8 Platoon arrived in our position with a 2" mortar. As they had no sights for the weapon, by a series of trials and errors, they landed half a dozen bombs in the enemy area nearest Lieut Yates' position. The group with the white flag coming towards us were met and motioned to drop all their equipment and it appeared to us as if they were being fired on by their own men from the other flank. As there were several among them who were wounded and being carried or helped, we quickly moved them to our rear and sent them off under 2 guards towards Company HQ. While I was despatching these POWs, Corporal Curr called out that another "Jerry" had stood up and was coming towards us.

I walked out to meet him in front of our position and he requested he be taken to our Commanding Officer as he and his men wanted to surrender.

The 2" mortar men had been doing a good job and had landed about ten 2" bombs almost in the German's ditch. This seemed to demoralise them as they stopped firing. I directed the "Hun" officer to where Lieut Yates was and he headed off in that direction. He spoke good English and I said he could surrender to me, but that seemed to offend him as he stuck his head in the air and said "I will only surrender to one of your officers". I didn't care, he could have surrendered to general Morshead if he liked, as long as he surrendered, as we were out of ammo.

At about this time I noticed one of our Carriers with a Vickers mounted on it coming up on our right flank. He was up on a slight rise and was about 150 yards away and moved to a position where he could fire right down the ditch enfilading the Germans. That soon made their minds up, and after a few long bursts the Germans started standing up in groups all along the ditch. At this point Lieut Cobb arrived with some more ammo which we hastily handed out and prepared to carry out our little war. The Jerries thought otherwise though, and they surrendered, from memory about 80 odd. They gave no trouble, we made them drop all of their arms and equipment and marched them up to Company Head Quarters.

They were a full Coy from a Machine Gun Battalion and had ridden through the perimeter defences on the tanks. When the tanks had been fired upon by the RHA, the troops, took cover in a half dug tank ditch, which made a good trench from which to fight. As to the Mortars the only one used was the 2" from 8 Platoon and the carrier was commanded by Tom Keys – I think he was a sergeant at that that time. A rather remarkable thing was that 9 Platoon did not suffer one casualty, but there were certainly a few near misses. I believe one of the Bren gunners in Lieut Yates' group shot the German Commander, a Lieut Colonel [Ponath] through the neck and killed him and that seemed to demoralise the Jerries. They covered him in a big Swastika flag when we cleaned up the area.

It was surprising to me from the amount of equipments the Germans had and the number of men available, that they didn't offer more resistance. I suppose the fact that their tanks had struck such stiff opposition, and then shot through, left them with a feeling of isolation and being surrounded, looking as though we knew what we were about (which we didn't). I suppose they thought the position was hopeless anyway. It was our first experience of fire, and there was no one more pleased than me when they decided to call it a day. I remember Bill Cobb saying on the way back to our lines "Robbie you say you don't think you had a casualty, well Christ that's beginner's luck". This would be perhaps the first German defeat.

REPORT ON PATROL

Capt AG Smith, 2/15 Bn war diary, 14 April 1941

After an attack on 14th April 41 at approx. 0730 hrs (CSM) Sgt Robinson reported to me that men were seen by RHA getting into an anti-tank ditch near the vicinity of some disabled tanks.

I immediately got in touch with BHQ and obtained permission to send out a platoon to contact the party.

At approx. 0900 hrs No 9 Pl, A Coy under Lieut Yates a total strength of 31 men with CSM Robinson as guide set out to contact the men.

The party advanced in open formation for about 800 yds when 2 enemy (Germans) came out of the Anti-Tank ditch to surrender. As Mr Yates went forward to take the prisoners the remainder of the enemy who were in two groups opened cross fire with machine guns. The men were then dispersed one section to the right under cover of a sand hill (two men in the ditch were left with the prisoners) one section was placed on the forward part of the ditch which is 3V3 shaped [probably 3ft deep and 3 yds wide] to keep the enemies' heads down. Mr Yates took another section forward into the ditch when they were held up. Observing no movement for about 20 minutes I contacted BHQ and asked for assistance, the Pl of this Coy being under fire. Meanwhile a runner reported back to report the position and ask for assistance.

Two carriers came out and one opened fire on one of the enemy parties which were in the right sector which immediately surrendered.

The remainder, approx 76 in number, opened fire on prisoners and carrier. The 2 mortars with the PL fired into the group in the ditch and this was very effective shortly after which the prisoners surrendered. Enemy casualties were 3 killed (including the commander[Ponath]) and 14 wounded some seriously injured. 100 men were taken prisoners and this Pl[atoon] suffered no casualties whatever.

Mr Yates and the section with him acted with cool determination and courage and the capture of these prisoners saved a probable assault on the

25pdr battery and this company at nightfall. The enemy were exceptionally well equipped with a very large number of automatic weapons, anti tank rifles and stick bombs, binoculars and pistols and about 30 rifles.

[AG Smith] Capt
OC A Coy 2/15 Bn

REPORT OF CARRIER ACTION

Sgt JT Keys, 2/15 Bn war diary, 14 April 1941

Acting under instructions from CEHA HQ, I reported at A Coy with two Bren Gun Carriers where I collected 4 men and two 2" Mortars. I was informed by the OC of A Coy that two Platoons were held up ... and had gone to ground. The strength of the enemy was unknown, but it was known that they possessed a number of MG's[machine guns].

On arrival at the position we unloaded the 2" Mortars and crews behind a convenient knoll, as the enemy kept up a steady fire from behind cover of a long trench which ran at right angles to the knoll. This trench was originally dug for a pipe line and extended for some distance, and it was apparent at once that with a Carrier at each and we would dominate the position. Whilst the mortars engaged the enemy the carriers under instructions from myself went to each end of the trench where excellent enfilade fire was obtained. When moving around the flanks one Carrier was hit with an A/Tk Rifle which was found to be jammed after capture.

When the enemy found that they were trapped they stood up and surrendered with the exception of two who rushed back into the trench and re-commenced firing. These were dealt with and this stopped further resistance: enemy casualties – 3 killed, 7 badly wounded, 3 slightly wounded, captured 87.

JT Keys Sgt
4Pl 2/15 Bn AIF

NAZI VEHICLE RECOGNITION FLAG TAKEN AT TOBRUK

Australian War Memorial, Canberra (REL3973)

Following the donation of this Nazi vehicle-recognition flag to the AWM, curator Greg Goddard compiled a description and a history of that banner which can be accessed electronically on the AWM website. Made in Germany, the red, cotton flag displays on the front centre. but not on the reverse side, a black and white swastika. Blood and grease stains remain on both sides.

This flag was presented to Capt Alfred Greig Smith (QX6199) as victor by members of A Coy, 2/15 Bn on 14 April 1941 after Lt Ron Yates' platoon and two carrier crews captured nearly 100 members of Rommel's crack 8 Machine Gun Bn. That action is described in Kevin Robinson's recollections and the two reports which precede this article.

At the end of the battle, the German commander, Lt-Col Gustav Ponath, was killed. The flag was ceremoniously draped over his body before he was buried temporarily at an unknown site. In March 2011, it was distinctly displayed as a brightly-lit centrepiece of an exhibition at AWM in Canberra to mark the 70th anniversary of the siege of Tobruk.

OBSERVATIONS OF A COY AT EL ADEM ROAD

Sgt HS (Tony) Rowan, Tobruk diary, 1941

15 April 1941: Major Craig from 13th Battalion is now in Command. Capt McKewan is 2/IC, Lt Guest is Adj, Lt Jenkinson to Capt, Robinson CCMQ Company, Don Parker now has 12 Platoon. W Kelly came to us for a while and then went to 11 Platoon, B Coy. W Cobb is now 2/IC A Coy and Capt Smith is OC. Dave Scroggins is now OC 7 Platoon. I got the biggest fright I ever had in the Army, they tried to make me CO of MQ Coy but I kicked up a fuss so they let me go back to my Platoon! They said they wanted a man with good organising ability but I said I was a soldier not a grocer!

We have seen a great deal of fighting in the last few days and we all seem to take it all right. There was a great battle yesterday morning and our Company took 90 prisoners – all Germans. We are the first troops to bump the Germans in this War. Tanks, AFV's, troops, guns and aeroplanes all took part yesterday. We saw planes shot down yesterday in front of us and I saw one pilot bail out. 21 enemy planes against three of ours was the day's tally, 9 tanks and 23 AFVs and about 500 prisoners. Our position is now about 200 yards in front of the Battery of 25 lb guns and the boys cheer like hell when they get stuck into their tanks. One tank got to within 200yds of us but then turned back.

The boys got dozens of souvenirs including lugers and binoculars. We saw a great battle of tanks about three days ago; it seems a pity to see the planes shot down, they look so pretty in the air. The battle yesterday morning was fought at about 6am. Started in a bitter howling gale and dust storm and it was hard to tell friend from foe. This is the coldest hole of a place I have ever seen and the wind is awful. The German gear is splendid and we have got one of their Lolly guns and find it far better than the Bren. The Bren is absolutely useless in sandy country and only jams when most wanted. Damn rifle jams also, and you have to flick it open with your foot.

The Italians' gear is more showy and not as good as the Jerry's. The binoculars are very powerful and the Luger pistol is a very fine job. Have just heard that Lt Doug Cubitts was killed yesterday. I think he was at school with Andrew [Rowan at Church of England Grammar School, East Brisbane]. The British gunners are wonderful chaps and stick to their guns to the last. They are very accurate and blow the tanks right off the ground. I have actually seen them hit tanks, one hit is enough.

ACCOUNT OF THE MOP-UP IN LETTER HOME TO MILES, QUEENSLAND

Pte Morgan Munckton, newspaper cutting, unknown source, 1941, AG Smith collection

Digger ML Munckton writes interestingly of adventures in Tobruk in a letter to his mother at Miles, Q'ld.

"You should just see the fireworks at night," he writes. "Often the place is lit up like day. Tracer shells from our anti-aircraft guns shoot into the sky in colours of red, green and white, and searchlights send up beams of white light until all overhead is sparkling and aglow.

Gun flashes and tracer bullets add to the blaze. Latter are filled with a chemical that burns red, and the bullets look like red hot coals flying through the air. When thousands of them are in the air at once, Guy Fawkes night has nothing on the display.

Easter Monday, about daylight, the Germans launched an attack which was broken up. After the tanks and planes had retreated, 36 of us were sent out to take prisoner any of the tank crews we could find.

We came across a party of Germans hiding behind a stone barricade. We didn't know they were there until they opened fire on us and the bullets started whistling around. It was funny the way it happened. Some of our chaps were inspecting a tank when bullets began to ping on the sides on it like a lot of bees buzzing. It was a few seconds before we realised someone was shooting on us. Then we made a dash across open ground to get under cover and unexpectedly landed in the same trench as the enemy. However, they didn't hit any of our fellows, and, after a couple of hours banging away at each other, we took 104 prisoners.

Those were the first German prisoners captured by the AIF in the war.

chapter 9

OBSERVATIONS ON LIFE AT TOBRUK TO JULY 1941

CORRESPONDENCE ON PEOPLE, EVENTS AND CONDITIONS

Lieut Ron A Yates, correspondence, April-June 1941, W. Yates, Toowoomba

April 12th As you can see by the date, it is now eight days since I started this letter, as things started far more suddenly than I expected, and in that time, I have not had any sleep, and it has been impossible to get any mail away. Our Battalion has had a bit of a knock. I cannot give you any details until it is published, but I want you to know and let Mother know I am safe, as I am one of the lucky ones. I may be unable to get mail away regularly, but I know you will understand.

There is no doubt about Australians. At one stage when things were nasty, I went round my men to calm them down, and found them playing poker, as if they were at a picnic. I hope you forgive the disjointed letter, as I am writing it and trying to watch the enemy at the same time. However, don't worry about me as I'll be as safe as a house. I must close now, as I have to go on watch. Remember that no news is good news.

April 16th Goodness knows when this letter will reach you, as we are still in the thick of things, and I do not think any mail will either come or get away until after this show is finished, also if this letter is a bit jerky, I would explain that at the moment the old "Hun" is shelling us heavily, and I do not mind admitting that I am not as comfortable as I might be.

Well, I am now seasoned to war, as we did a fair job a day or two ago. I can't skite to you as much as I would like to, owing to censorship regulations, but my Platoon was given the very doubtful honour of rounding up a German raiding party so out we went, thirty-two of us and were surprised to find the German strength was 110 fully armed men, with every type of modern equipment. Two of them surrendered as a decoy to us, and when I went forward to search them, the remainder opened up with machine guns. I scattered my men and gradually closed in on them. We fought for five hours, and then their Commander came out with a white flag. I went forward to him. He spoke English, so I told him to bring all his men out with hands up, which he did much to my relief, as I was a bit windy that he might have been another decoy and the first machine guns went too close for my liking. However, the outcome was that we killed five, wounded twelve, and took prisoners ninety-three, and we didn't lose one man either wounded or killed.

We also got a lot of valuable equipment, a few trucks of it, and I now have equipped myself with two marvellous German pistols and two of the best make of German field glasses, one 8x30 and one 10x50. You can tell your father I will give them to him after the war, as they are better than his. One of the Germans, an officer [Capt Bartsch] came to see me. He was crying and asked if he could speak with his Captain before he died, so I took him over, but had to turn my back. The Captain died a few minutes later, and he covered him with a Swastika, made a smart about turn, gave the Nazi salute, and came to me with tears rolling down his cheeks, and said "Now I await your command". I was terribly touched, and could not feel bitter about it, and gave them water before I handed them over.

It is a strange thing, as always I imagined I would be windy in a scrap, and that if I got prisoners I would shoot them all, but I was exactly opposite, as I was never calmer in my life than when we were fighting, and after the fight, I only felt pity for them. Perhaps it was because none of my men were hurt.

My Platoon are a marvellous lot of blokes. I will never forget the way they acted, and they carried out all my instructions implicitly. They are terribly funny. One cove did not have a rifle, and he came and told me about it, and another bloke said "You will be uphill alright, as you haven't even got teeth to bite the swine with." (This cove had false teeth). Another bloke had a letter from his girl's sister in which she said "Doreen has not heard from you for over six weeks, and is terribly cut up, so if you have found someone over there that you like better, be a man and write and tell her." This bloke brought me the letter and said – "What would you do in a case like that. I haven't even seen a woman for three months. She must think I am touring the Continent."

April 18th We have just received congratulations from the GOC. It appears one of the Germans killed was a Colonel [Ponath]. I have been recommended for something, but do not expect anything. A runner has just arrived to tell me that Douglas Cubitt left us a few days ago. It's terrible, there may be a chance of Bill Hart returning to us, but Doug has gone for good. I am not allowed to write yet to tell you about it, but when I am able to, it will be to their parents. Whatever you do, don't worry about me as I am quite safe. I have not been getting many letters. I know I won't get any here, but even before this started I did not get many, my letters must be going astray.

April 20th More mail arrived yesterday, and I missed out again. I have missed three times now. Our new CO [Cragg] seems a good sort of cove, but no one could ever come up to Colonel Marlan, the last words the old CO said to me were – "How are your wife and son Yates.' He was always asking after you. Somehow I seem to feel he will turn up again too some day. Anyway I have a Hun colonel to my credit, and a Captain and Five Lieutenants prisoners to make up for some of our boys.

Today is a miserable day. It is raining and cold as blazes. I have a bit of covering over my dug out, but every now and then the rains drips through. However the enemy have been very quiet all day, which is a relief, but it makes one a bit suspicious when he is quiet. Had bit of a shock early – a plane with our markings came over. No one took any notice until three bombs dropped. However, the Air force just rang up to apologise, as something happened to their bomb rack, and the pilot had to drop his bombs. We have seen a lot of planes in fights lately, and I have seen a lot of planes shot down. They have been mostly enemy though, as our coves seem to have it well over them here. The other morning five were shot down within half a mile of us in about five minutes.

April 30th Well, things are much the same here. I'm still in the front line. The Huns have made two more large attacks here, but have been driven back, each time with severe losses. However, they seem to have countless numbers, and you do one bunch up and straight away another take their place. They seem to have no thought for manpower at all. I haven't had an actual scrap since the one on Easter Monday morning, when we did that crowd up, but we have been under shell fire all the time. Under machine gun fire part of the time and every day the German air force pays us a visit. They come over 100 at a time and play hell for about an hour and then go home again. I am beginning to lose faith in the German as a fighter. I think he is over estimated.

They win because there is always so many of them, but with numbers equal they are not in the race.

The Englishmen here are a wonderful crowd of fellows. The officers are very bored young men, but cool and calm and the Tommies (mostly Cockneys) are delightful. They believe anything you tell them, and believe me our blokes tell them anything. You would laugh if you could hear our coves describing life in Australia to them. However they think our coves are great and follow them about all day. The type of Englishman that is over here we seldom meet in Australia, they are a great lot, most of them fought in France, and they are most efficient at their job.

[Lt A] McDonald is now left and gone back to a job at base, so the old Battalion is a lot different from when we left Redbank, and without old Colonel Marlan, it can never be the same.

7 May 1941 I am now permitted to give you the news. 8 officers, Colonel Marlan, Major Barton, Major [Ronald] Rosier, Neal Currie, Bill Hart, John Linton, Bob Donovan and the Padre [Rev CS Arkell], 9 sergeants, including the RSM Arthur Cotman and 148 privates were all cut off by the enemy who were in tanks and armoured fighting vehicles, and have not been heard of since. The only information we have received came from one man who escaped and he told us that the last he saw of them all was that they were surrounded by tanks and A.F.V.'s who were firing on them with machine guns, so that is all we know actually although we are hoping that they are still alive and prisoners.

You can realise what a blow it was to our old battalion, as practically all battalion headquarters with all our records etc were amongst those missing, also the pay sergeant with all our money and records, so the old Huns are probably having a few parties at our expense.

I was a bit lucky, as I was one of those who were last to leave and we were to fight a rear guard action and delay the Huns whilst these others escaped. However, the Huns went around the back and attacked the front of the convoy instead of us in the rear, and when we came through the road, the Huns were on, was closed, and we came through on another track.

Every day I become more of a fatalist, first of all Battalion HQ, the ones who should be safer than any of us, are taken prisoner, and then Douglas [Cubitt] who had one of the safest jobs is gone. The rest of us were in the thick of the fighting all the time and didn't get a scratch, and poor old Doug and another cove was sent out by the Brigadier to have a look after the battle was over, and they both got knocked over by a machine gun.

Things are much the same here. The Huns have made several attempts to push through, but they have been driven back each time with heavy losses. A funny thing happened the other night, one of the English Officers was out on patrol, and he was captured by some Germans. The Germans got lost in the dark and instead of going back to their own lines finished up in ours, and were taken prisoner.

These English coves are marvellous types and wonderful soldiers. One of them the other night wanted to find out where the German artillery was firing from, so he climbed on top of a truck where he knew they could see him, so they would fire on him, and then he would take a bearing from the flashes of their guns, Sure enough the enemy opened fire, and dropped shells all round him. I yelled out to him that he had better get down and he said "but really old man they are frightful shots these Huns what". However, he calmly took his bearings and then strolled down, rang up his battery and gave them the bearings and in a few seconds, over came our shells, and they blew the German guns to pieces.

The German prisoners I have struck are fine looking fellows. Most of them, but very cold and arrogant. When we got a bunch of prisoners one of the officers had two bullet holes in him, and I told him he'd better go in the truck. He said: "No, I walk". He walked but collapsed before he got to HQ. It seems a pity that two such races should kill each other off, while the mongrels remain at home and look on. It seems awful to me.

These English have a marvellous sense of humour. I could listen to them all day. They are cool coves, most of them, but you would like them, and laugh at them. ..... They are not the feeble type that we see in Australia mostly.

13 May The Huns are still throwing everything they have got at us without success. They are reported to have thousands of Italians behind them, well behind them I am afraid. It is a really beautiful at night, the various lights that light the whole sky, tracer bullets, flares and searchlights looking for planes, it would almost be enjoyable if it was not for the explosion that follows. The only thing that worries me is the shells. I don't mind planes as you can see them coming. We have about 70 over four times a day and we almost look forward to them, as you just go to ground if they are too close to be comfortable, and you are safe as a house, also with machine guns, you can take cover, and have a crack at them, and unless they get you with their first burst you are reasonably safe, but the shells – all you hear is the whine followed by an explosion –all of them seem to be coming straight at you, and when you look up they are sometimes half a mile away. The old hands say there is no need to worry about the ones you hear, as they have gone past you before you hear them, it's the ones you don't hear that cause all damage, they may be right, but being of a cautious nature I still bite the dust in a hurry when I hear a whine, however our artillery is far superior to theirs, so I think they are getting more than they are giving us. However, the shelling goes on all day, so I am gradually getting used to it.

18 May Well I am still in Tobruk, and slowly going mad through boredom. It is just a matter of waiting for the Huns to attack – drive them back and wait for them to attack again. We go out occasionally at night, and do them up and come home again. They are just as jittery as can be and are frightened of Australians and don't like night work much. Most of the Germans fight fair, but the dagoes [Italians] are a dirty lot, they come out with hands up and as soon as you get close enough to reach them, but whilst they are out of your range they fire – they also put their hands up and when you walk up they throw grenades, but we are gradually getting them out of that by doing them up with bayonets.

28 May We are still back in reserve, but we are kept fairly busy although things have been fairly quiet. I had a marvellous swim the other day, spent the day swimming and lying in the sun on the beach, it was great, and I got rid of all the lice and dirt that I had accumulated during the last eight weeks. However, the next day we had a dreadful dust storm, so it did not take long to get back to normal again.

The other day, two Englishmen escaped from a German prison camp dressed as Arabs. It took them thirty five days to get here, and the Arabs fed them during that time. They told me they had seen Colonel Marlan in the prison, they said that our other missing men were there also, and they had been treated very well, and had received the same food as the Germans had, and that arrangements had been made for all the officers to be flown to Germany by 'plane but just as they were about to leave, the RAF bombed the aerodrome and smashed up a lot of the troop carrying planes, and at the time they escaped the officers were still in the prison camp, although they had probably gone by now.

31 May ... you are a beast for not believing it all about the German raiding party we did up on Easter Monday. I really did not exaggerate any of it, so you can tell your friends if you want to, as a matter of a fact, the only reason I did not exaggerate was I was frightened it might be censored by someone I know. As it turned out, I left out some of the more spectacular details. The effort was mentioned in the "Tobruk Truth", the following day, and took up three paragraphs, which was not bad considering the "Tobruk Truth" comprises one page the size of a writing pad. Both the General and Brigadier sent messages of congratulations, as we were the first to get to ... with and beat the Germans, all other prisoners which had been taken were Italians up till then, and they do not count for much, and on top of that they outnumbered us 3 to 1. They were dug in and we had to advance on them in the open while they were firing at us all the time, while I had no other officer with me and took that Colonel and officers etc as prisoners. I was recommended too, that was the truth, but still I do not think I will get anything, as in my report I sort of took the attitude that I was used to doing such things every day, and it really was a very modest statement.

May 29th Well yesterday we were relieved from the front line for a few days so will get a swim before we go back to the line again. However, that is about the only advantage this place has, as the dust is terrific here. You can only see about 10 yards in front of you, and they shell the place a bit.

Last night I spent in chasing rats. The rats here are over two feet long and were running all over me, so I got out my pistol and spent the night having pot shots at them. In no time I had all the Company officers in to see what was going on. I think old Greg [sic] Smith (our Captain now Alec Ralston is transferred to another Coy), thought I had a Hun in my room. When he saw the dead rats scattered about the place he abused me. He is a grand cove, old Greg. I think he is one of the most honest men I have ever met. He is just an ordinary sort of bloke but a fellow that could not do you a bad turn if he tried, and as straight as can be. He is very popular. Bill Cobb is second in command of our Company, and is a Captain. ... Lance Bode is a captain also, and is in command of C Company, so I am gradually working my way up the seniority list, all promotions are made by the length of time you have had a

Commission in the AIF. So as I got in about three weeks after all the others, I have got a bit to go yet.

The men are very bitter on the men who are in Australia and who have not joined up. I don't blame them either, when I think of Greg Smith with two children – married before the war broke out, and masses of others out here, and then I think of a German officer I took prisoner – a fine looking cove, straight as a ramrod and absolutely fearless. One of my men grabbed his wallet, in which was a photo of his Mother and his wife. He came to me and said "Please if your man wants a souvenir he can have my Iron Cross that I won in France, or he can keep my wallet, but would you mind asking him if he would return the photograph of my wife and Mother, it is all I have left." No doubt there are many coves like this German on both sides, trying to do each other in and they [stay] safe at home with the women and children. There is only one thing in war that is any good at all, and that is the comradeship of men like those I have mentioned.

5th June 1941 Well I am back again at the front. This time only 300 yards from "Jerry", but things are fairly quiet. We snipe at each other occasionally, and it is more like what I imagined war would be. The other day the "Jerries" waved a red cross, and one cove yelled out and asked if we could have a four hour truce while their Ambulance came and collected their wounded, so I told them it would be all right, so they got out of their holes, and we got out of ours, and we had a yarn across "no man's land", and as soon as the Ambulance left we waved to each other and jumped back into our holes, and got to it again. By the way that is the truth although it sounds ridiculous, in fact all war seems ridiculous although I suppose it must be.

We have another CO [Lt Col R Ogle] now who seems a decent sort of cove, and is straightening everybody up. We had a bad time for a long while .... the cove who took Colonel Marlan's place [Major TF Cragg] ... has gone back to base now and this new bloke looks a good type. He has only been here a few days, but he did not take long to pull the blokes together, and let them know who is boss. However, we will never get another Colonel Marlan, who I think is one of the best coves I have ever met. Old Greg Smith (my OC) has gone to hospital. He has been sick for a long time and got worse when we were in reserve. He would not go to hospital for a long time, the silly cow said that the blokes would think he did not like the front. However, in the end they made him go. He kicked up a fuss but they made him go. He said he would be back in a few days, but I don't think he will, as I can never understand how he passed the Doctor in the first place.

June 6th Nothing much has been happening except sitting and waiting. I'll be nuts if I have to stop here much longer. You never see anyone and cannot move until dark, and everyone is starting to get one everyone else's nerves. However, I suppose we will have to put in another fortnight .... We are up all night, every night, and you cannot sleep during the day owing to the heat and the flies. The only consolation is that the Huns must be feeling it more than we are, as they are not used to it. The Canteen service here is rotten, the only people who seem to do any good for the lads is the Salvation Army probably because there is no politics connected with it, I will never throw off at the old Salvoes again, as out here they do a wonderful job. .... I wish they would find a decent place to fight a war, instead of picking what must be the worst place in the world. Julia Creek is paradise compared with this.

June 11th A lot of the coves have been suffering from dysentery, but so far I have been fortunate although I have had to send a lot of men back with it. It is a terrible thing to get. You cannot move about during the day, and have to stay in the trenches during the day with the sun streaming down on you. The heat is like Winton was when we were there, but the flies are terrible, I have never seen so many in my life. .... We throw everything at each other from daylight until about 10.30, when it starts to get hot and then both the Germans and ourselves appear to have a mutual agreement, that it is getting too hot and not a shot is fired until about 6 o'clock in the evening, then we go flat out again until about 9 o'clock, when it gets dark. Then we carry on with spasmodic firing all through the night. It is really funny how everyone stops firing about 10 pm. Sometimes one cove on either side will fire a stray shot after 10 o'clock, and you will hear someone in the enemy lines yell out "Don't you ever eat over there?" Or sometimes they will fire and one of our coves will yell something back at them about their watches or clocks being wrong. The other night we could hear them wheeling a wheel barrow or something about, and it was squeaking pretty badly, and one of our coves called out "Put some oil on that noisy thing, we want to go to sleep." They yelled something back that I did not hear, and then all the smug coves started singing in English "We will hang out our washing on the [Siegfried] line." ....

Old Greg Smith has gone back to base. I do not think he will come back. I miss him as he was a grand old cove. However, Bill Cobb has taken his place and is doing a good job. Bill is one of the few coves that promotion improves ..., being cool and calm.

If only a few of our planes would come over occasionally it would make such a difference, but we have not even seen one of our planes for over two months and every day about 60 or 70 enemy planes calmly fly over us and do as they like, without any opposition. .... However, with all their advantage in the air, they will never beat us here. They have had a few good cracks and have been knocked back each time.

COMMENTS ON LIFE AT TOBRUK

Sgt R Cowie, 'Bob Cowie's story', *CH*, pp. 207-12

It was during the siege that Lord Haw Haw [William Joyce] became a (popular?) radio commentator with special messages for the garrison. The Berlin radio made a mistake in trying to scare the Aussies into surrendering. The longer the odds offered by Haw Haw the more the Aussies backed themselves – the odds were long; the fighting would be hard but they knew the stakes. The more scornful Haw Haw became the more important became the job of the defenders. As far as morals went it would have been far better for Goebbels to ignore the garrison altogether. It had the effect of lifting morale instead of lowering it and, according to the British Field Censor, the spirit of troops' mail from Tobruk was much higher than that of other parts of the Western Desert. Apparently this was a result of so much attention being focussed on the fortress by the broadcasts.

Mentioned only briefly in previous parts of this story were other dangers associated with the siege – other than air raids, shelling, German and Italian attacks, booby traps and minefields and other forms of hardware. The climate was healthy enough after Italian rubbish and filth had been cleared away – apart from the dust. The heat was dry and the nights cool. The dust storms were severe and were a trial, being worse in Tobruk than the open desert. Inside the perimeter thousands of wheels of vehicles had churned the dust into a fine powder which was whipped up into a choking cloud by the faintest wind. Dust was breathed and dust blotted out everything but still the manning of posts, guns and the perimeter continued.

Next to dust it is difficult to decide between flies and fleas as the next greatest pest. There was very little animal life other than little brown mice, some big rats in the caves, a number of starved Libyan dogs, a few cats, some jackals and gazelles, jerboa, a couple of goats and one ancient sheep. This last animal known as "Larry the lamb" was a mascot of a British Ack Ack Battery and jealously guarded for it is said the gunners placed a sentry on him at night to protect him from marauding Aussies.

It is reported that there was no mosquito problems and so this obviated the risk of malaria. Dysentery was a troublesome illness but as long as the troops drank chlorinated water and strictly observed sanitary regulations it was kept in check. However "carelessness' (or was it circumstances?) caused several severe outbreaks, the worst being in June when 226, plus others in the line, were down with the complaint – three times as many as there were battle casualties. Later, after four months, deficiencies in rations began to make their mark.

In the first three months there were no fresh and very little tinned vegetables or fruit. The bakeries produced reasonably good bread six days a week and this and bully beef and biscuits were the main form of sustenance. When the bakeries were bombed it was bully and biscuits all round for all ranks. Variety of bully was introduced by tinned meat and vegetables (M&V), stew, tinned bacon and tinned herrings ("gold fish") which I believe large numbers will not eat to this day. Margarine was rationed but sugar and jam more so. Vitamin C in the form of ascorbic tablets made up in some small way for fresh greens and fruit. After several months on this diet troops suffered from desert sores – scratches that became infected and took weeks to heal. By the time the troops got back to Palestine the average weight loss was two stone.

The figures for shock cases (bomb happy) are interesting. Of 207 cases treated at the hospital, 38% returned to their units without leaving Tobruk, 23% became fit for front line service after treatment in Palestine, 23% became fit for only base duties, 12% were returned to Australia permanently and only 3% were found to be malingerers. The 4th AGH was bombed 17 times and at least one attack was deliberate. Another hospital was set up on the beach a few hundred yards from an Ack Ack position and other targets and was bombed and strafed several times in the two weeks, one attack was deliberate and it was then moved two miles along the beach and was not subject to further attack. Generally the Germans respected the Red Cross and regimental Aid Posts but we remember two hospital ships in the harbour were subjected to a dive bombing attack which resulted in them being sunk. Troops swimming and sun baking on the beaches were frequently machine gunned and would mount Bren guns as Ack Ack defences.

Troops quartered in town were the most comfortable when taking all circumstances into account. They certainly had to withstand frequent bombings and occasional shells but they also could build solid shelters, sleep in deep tunnels dug by the Italians and timber up rooms in stone houses to make them so strong that a direct hit would be necessary to disturb them. They also had the advantages of good swimming, setting up their home-made distilleries to provide good drinking water (and probably other beverages) and boosting their rations with fish caught by the "grenade method". The troops in the zone between this town and the perimeter, which included the various headquarters, were the next in comfort because they were more or less static. Worse off, by far, were the Australian infantry who moved every couple of weeks from the Red Line concrete posts to exposed Blue Line positions, then to an inner reserve position and then the Salient. Except for those who could distil salt water there was little water for the troops in general. That water was brackish and did little to moisten a dust-encrusted set of tonsils. The ration was half a gallon of water a day for all purposes: cooking, drinking and whatever you could do with it. ....

Water was short to say nothing of beer. A newspaper cutting which trickled in with some mail made reference to the fact that beer was regularly supplied to the troops in the garrison. This particularly annoyed the troops who well and truly proved that Aussies don't require beer in order to do a job in war and a well done job at that. Canteen supplies and mail were most important. Various reports refer to the quantities of both delivered in and out of Tobruk. The Australian Postal Unit operated from a bank building and in August was handling 50 tons of incoming mail weekly, mostly for Australians and 5000 parcels from the Australian Comforts Fund. (These parcels were distributed to all troops in Tobruk and not only to Australians). The outgoing mail in the bulk consisted of souvenirs made by troops, Stuka, Italian shell cases, hand grenades and 'general wreckage".

Cigarettes were almost as valuable as mail. In the British ration there was a free issue of 50 per week, but there was always a shortage and many and varied were the recipes used to produce some of the "makings". By September the ration was increased by Canteen supplies. There were always an over abundance of volunteers to unload ships such as Canteen supplies. Maybe there was a chance of getting away with some of the cargo. One story goes of a battalion working party getting away with so much cargo that they were denied the privilege [of] providing unloading parties. A similar type of "scrounging" took place around food dumps but this was not caused by front line troops. All the fat boys belonged to base areas and could be an explanation of some reports relating to plenty of food being available throughout the siege.

As in all warfare, news was a major factor. Rumours are great morale busters and this resulted in the daily newssheet edited and published by Sgt WH Williams, "Tobruk Truth – Dinkum Oil" being produced. Each night Sgt Williams listened to the ABC, took shorthand notes and "local" news extracts from Australian newspapers and typed the items on a waxed stencil and roneod-off copies on an antiquated cyclostyle machine. At first his radio and other equipment was Italian in origin. When it looked like breaking down a new typewriter and duplicator were sent up from Cairo and the Comforts Fund provided a new radio. The daily circulation was 600 and because of paper shortage (just another shortage) the news was printed on the back of Italian Army forms. Some Australian units also produced a newssheet, They were the 2/23rd Battalion's "Mud and Blood": the 2/24th 's "Furphy Flier" and 2/48th's "Grubbs Gazette".

It is true to say even with "Tobruk Truth – Dinkum Oil" etc that a lot of the troops did not know what was going on inside the garrison. In September the 20th Brigade Concert Party put on a concert that ran for four nights. It was held in a man-made cave tunnelled in rock by the Italians in a wadi near the El Adem crossroads. It had a concrete floor, a stage consisting of a rough wooden platform draped with army blankets and camouflage nets; the footlights were car headlamps in cut-aeay kerosene tins, the "hall" was 20 yards wide and 50 yards long. The players and audience were in the line a few days earlier and were both grimy and dusty with steel helmets and rifles slung over the shoulder. The concert was taped by [war correspondent] Chester Wilmot and eventually broadcast by the ABC. The accompaniment was a piano, saxophone, violin, piano accordion and a mouth organ. With the exception of the latter, the instruments had a history. The piano had once been played on the piazza of the "Albergo Tobruch" for perfumed Italian officers dressed in silk lined velvet collared uniforms as they danced with their painted ladies; the saxophone had been heard in Brisbane's Tivoli Theatre before the war and its owner Ted Donkin, is reported to have carried it to the borders of

Tripolitania and back again and had it wrapped in a blanket and buried it the sand to keep the dust out of it. The violin's ancestry is in extreme doubt and because of another shortage (catgut this time) was strung with sig wire. The saxophone did not thrive in the dust and developed an attack of leakage of the lungs or asthma which was rectified when it reported to the RMO who applied sticking plaster poultices to the injured parts.

The only thing shared by all were the flies, fleas, dust, bully beef and biscuits (bully beef will be remembered being approx 12 oz to the tin and eight "dog" biscuits per packet). There was much hard work and general activity for any real boredom to set in for any length of time. Most "spare time" was devoted to weapon maintenance, "manufacturing" such things as ammo and tobacco and when time permitted the odd bit of scrounging – a great Aussie habit.

Mines and "booby traps" produced a horror all of their own. Casualties would have been much greater were it not for the excellent delousing work of the 2/13 Field Engineer Company. On 29 June a patrol from 2/15 Battalion found a minefield just 200 yards forward of its own wire. Anti-personnel mines were exploded and an officer was killed. The explosion of the mine drew heavy machine gun fire and the patrol members flattened themselves on the ground they set off Jumping Jack mines with their three prongs which were the triggers to set off a primary charge blowing a nine pound mine packed with shrapnel some two feet in the air before it burst. Trip wires strung between camel thorn bushes were attached to booby traps. In their dugouts the Germans left various booby trap devices such as ammunition boxes which exploded a mine when moved.; what looked like cakes of soap pushed into the crevices between sand bags which exploded on being moved etc. The German positions were so heavily booby trapped that it was much safer to dig new positions than to occupy theirs. ....

Life in the Salient was one of discomfort to say the least. Dugouts were generally big enough to take two and three men only and, depending on the ground, could be up to four feet deep, roofed over with the strongest material that could be found in which bits of camel bush were tucked to try to make it blend with the desert and a bit more difficult for German snipers to find from 500 yards away. The dugouts were connected to short crawl trenches. By day the sun beat down transferring the dugout into a sweatbox into which the dust found its way creating a further clammy heat. And the fog of cigarette smoke and after some 13 hours of daylight it was a relief when night came and the cool fresh air could be breathed outside the dugout. Sleep by day was not always possible.

And with all that was the itchiness of lice, fly and flea bites and being generally dirty. It was not uncommon to have a "toilet" from about half a cup of water. First a quick clean of the teeth, then the shave and wipe over of the body with a damp face cloth or piece of towel. In some dugouts there was a primus of sorts which allowed for a "brew" during the day, but in others any tell-tale showing of smoke would draw enemy fire. At night a warm meal was delivered to the forward positions and usually was the same bully beef stew and prunes. There seemed to be an unwritten law on both sides for a couple of hours after darkness fell during which times both sides "replenished" their position but from midnight the "game" would be on again. "Exercise" was usually taken at night doing some wiring job, strengthening the defences or digging the crawl trenches a bit deeper. Others would take turns in the listening posts – a couple of hundred yards in no man's land in a slit trench fully 18 inches deep with eyes and ears straining and slowly growing cold from the desert chill. Then "stand to" and awaiting of dawn. Then the sequence would start again (unless there was an attack), probably some letter writing and very little "news", reading old magazines or books or just smoking the time away, if you had any smokes.

Appetites in general were not great. There was the "hot" meal at night but during the day there was no way in which anything could be cooked and the menu was limited – biscuits and margarine with a spot of jam or cheese; biscuits and cold tinned bacon; biscuits and cold bully beef; biscuits and cold meat and vegetables (M&V) or finally biscuits and gold fish (herrings), washed down with a gritty couple of drops of chlorinated water. (The Germans fared much better for their "captured" foodstuffs included chocolate, concentrated sugar, milk tablets, lemon drink, tablets etc.)

For the greater part of the siege troops went on patrol in what they had in the way of clothing but, after some months, patrols were equipped with special boots with thick rubber soles and special one piece patrol overalls with reinforced elbows and knees as protection against crawling over stony ground and through thorn bushes. Other socks were worn over the boots. Each man on patrol carried at least two or three grenades and as many automatic weapons as could be made available, the others were armed with rifle and bayonet. Mostly when patrols made a raid it was silent but a protective barrage was fired to help them in withdrawal. Many means were adopted to guide patrols home, single tracer bullets were fired from the post to which the patrol had to return. It is also reported that in one company of the 2/15th Battalion Ted Donkin often guided the men home to the front line posts by playing his saxophone. ....

As the Padre expressed Grace one day "For what we are about to eat, Thank God for the British Fleet". No doubt without British gunners – artillery, ack ack etc – and to the British Fleet, the garrison probably would have gone under. But of all the great work of the Royal Navy perhaps one, if not the most famous, of the small ships, was an Australian, Lt Alfred Palmer, known to everyone as "Pedlar". From May till October he skippered the 400 ton schooner "Maria Giovanni" which had been captured from the Italians and made a weekly run from Matruk to Tobruk. Frequently attacked from the air, his crew, with an assortment of scrounged anti-aircraft guns were successful in bringing down three enemy planes. It is stated that "Pedlar" found his way back to Tobruk harbour mostly by instinct or the ack ack fire. The entrance to the harbour was marked by two shielded lights and the Italians, finding this out, set up similar lights 15 miles to the East. One night in the dark and with no air raid to guide him into the harbour, "Pedlar" mistook the Italian lights for the harbour lights and sailed into a rocky section of the coast, "Maria Giovanni" was wrecked and "Pedlar" was taken prisoner. For his gallantry, he was awarded the Distinguished Service Cross.

NEWSPAPER REVIEW FOUR MONTHS DOWN THE TRACK

GEW Harrison, *Sydney Morning Herald* correspondent with the AIF, July 1941

The Rats of Tobruk

Grim Warfare in The Desert

For four months in the searing heat and blinding sandstorms of a North African summer the embattled garrison of Tobruk has clung like a poisoned thorn to the flank of the enemy drive against Egypt, forcing him to detach a greatly superior force to hold his dangerous threat in check and depriving him of the use of one of the few good harbours on this coast.

Ceaseless air raids – the total has now risen to one thousand – have been no more effective than the many attacks by tanks and infantry, and today the offensive spirit of the Australian, Indian and English troops who form the garrison is as strong as ever.

Behind the curt phrasing of the official communiqués, "offensive action by our patrols in the Tobruk area" lies a story of nightly daring sorties into the enemy lines of strong-points captured, losses inflicted, prisoners brought back, and above all, a sense of insecurity amounting a t times to panic amongst the Axis troops who have this tiger by the tail.

That unconsciously entertaining renegade, Lord Haw Haw, who can generally be depended on to provide the troops with something to laugh at, addresses periodic messages to the "Rats of Tobruk", as he has dubbed them by virtue of their underground habitations, inquiring tenderly after the welfare of "our self-supporting prisoners of war". Our men have appropriated the name with relish, and refer to themselves as "the rats", but the Axis troops who have felt the "rats'" teeth must find the humour wearing a bit thin.

As for being prisoners, they are not even completely besieged, because, despite the utmost efforts of enemy bombers and long-range naval guns, our ships, under the protection of the Mediterranean Fleet, still steam in and out of the harbour, bringing in supplies and reinforcements, evacuating wounded. Freighters have been sunk, hospital ships attacked, but the lifeline is still clear.

Graveyard of Ships

Set down in the midst of a desolate waste of sun-scorched sand, Tobruk exists by virtue of its harbour. It was quite a considerable town when the Italians held it – a town of little white and green cottages, with a group of big administrative buildings down near the wharves. Now shells and bombs, first from the RAF, later from Axis planes, have left a trail of shattered houses and uptorn streets, while the harbour itself is a graveyard of sunken ships, dominated by the grey hulk of the Italian cruiser *San Giorgio*.

As you steam into Tobruk harbour you do not see much sign of life – a few men bathing naked on a sheltered beach, the crews of anti-aircraft guns which have done such yeoman service and perhaps a scattered group round the quay. The defenders are farther out, in position behind the perimeter of barbed wire, concrete pillboxes and trenched which make up a semi-circle around the town and harbour. At these defences greatly superior Axis forces have been battering for four months, and they have got exactly nowhere. They have suffered heavy casualties, but our losses have been light.

Worse than shells and bombs are the flies and the sandstorms, but these are *condotterieri,* who owe no allegiance and attack friend and foe with magnificent impartiality. Flies settle everywhere in black evil swarms, and the air is always full of sand and dust. Sand is the seasoning with all meals; it blows into dugouts, swirls into sleeping quarters, and blots out the landscape for hours on end with choking brown pall. Ask any soldier serving there – friend or enemy – what is the worst feature of the siege, and he will reply, with some picturesque qualifying adjectives, "the sand".

No Food Shortage

There is no shortage of food, but equally there is no variety. The old Army standby, bully beef, does duty under a multitude of disguises. The lack of green vegetables is supplied by the issue of little tablets containing vitamin C. Drinking water is strictly rationed. Beer, of course, is unobtainable – the only real grievance the Australians have.

Despite, however, the difficult living conditions and the lack of variety in the menus, the troops are healthy and fit. There have been a few cases of sandfly fever and dysentery, and a little influenza, but there has been no outbreak of disease of any kind. As an officer put it, "The boys are in good nick, and their morale is a hundred percent" – they are in excellent spirits, and thoroughly confident.

When night comes the Tobruk rats show their fangs. Patrols, wearing sandshoes, all encumbering equipment left behind, creep silently through our wire into the enemy lines. To the watcher they seem to melt into the ground and disappear. It is quiet with the oppressive stillness of the desert night, and a young moon casts queer unreal shadows, and things seem to move where no things are.

Anxious minutes pass. There is the rat-tat-tat of a machine-gun, but this does not mean that they have been discovered – simply a nervous Italian gunner firing a burst "for luck". Suddenly from the enemy's lines come a wild shriek and a flurry of shots. More shots, spreading up and down the line, for the enemy's nerves are bad. Our patrols fight silently, using the bayonet and butt.

Work of Patrols

Patrols, which go out every night, are of two kinds, fighting and reconnaissance. The job of the reconnaissance patrol is to gather information, and, if possible, secure prisoners for identification and the members use all their bushcraft to avoid being discovered. A fighting patrol on the other hand, as its name implies, goes out to fight, to do as much damage and to kill as many of the enemy as possible. Its members will creep up on an enemy post, surround it, and then at a given signal rush it with the bayonet. There is a few minutes bloody work, and the whole thing is often over without a shot being fired.

Prisoners, who have evidently been fed on stores of Australian atrocities, are sullen and frightened when brought in. Frequently, although suffering from thirst, they refuse a drink from the proffered water bottles of their guards, apparently believing that it is an attempt to drug or poison them. The attitude of Italian and German officers to one another when in the same bunch of prisoners leaves no doubt of the bad terms on which the uneasy Axis bedfellows are.

So persistent, so successful, and so deadly have been our patrols that the enemy has been reduced to a state of almost panicky nervousness. He is in fact suffering from a bad state of the 'jitters', which leads him to put down artillery and mortar barrages on very slight provocation, and often indeed, on no provocation.

Fewer Germans Now

In the early weeks of the siege there was a considerable force of Germans engaged against Tobruk, and they launched several determined attacks, supported by tanks, in an attempt to smash through our defences. Our infantry let the tanks go through, to be dealt with by anti-tank guns posted in the rear, and then smashed the surprised German infantry, who had expected the tanks to clear the way for them. Latterly, however, it appears that the majority of Germans have been withdrawn, leaving the job to their doughty allies, the Italians (for whom the Germans make no effort to conceal their contempt), stiffened with German officers and NCO's.

German tanks, which played a big part in the earlier attacks on Tobruk, have had to be withdrawn to meet the British threat on the Sollum line, where we have taken a heavy toll of enemy armoured vehicles.

Now that the Italians have taken over the job of air attacks, they content themselves with high-level bombing. They never attempt to dive-bomb. Our casualties from air raids have been extraordinarily light, and for our troops the only real valued to the enemy of these air attacks, which are a daily occurrence, is nuisance value.

PART-TIME POETS
AG Smith collection

The Choice
Anon, *The Bulletin*

To leave all this, the vista of blue hills,
The sweep of gum-tips reaching to the sky.
The thrush's song as in its joy it spills
Its throbbing notes, and passes swiftly by.

To leave all this – the dear and homelike things
That with the years have more familiar grown,
Scarce noticed in life's rush – such potent strings
Are these to hold you back from the unknown.

To leave all this – soon to become
A tiny unit merged in war's vast scene,
Closing my soul to beauty – speechless – numb.
Forgetting all the things that might have been;

Living from day to day, from hour to hour,
The past erased, the future too unsure,
To ponder on. But were it in my power
I'd not draw back for all the glittering lure

Of safety. Better far to die and go
Out in the deeps, and leave behind
Me all the lovely things I used to know
Than live there with a conscious-haunted mind.

Who has not?
Sgt A Mitchell

Who has not heard the bullet crack?
Who has not passed a day
'Mongst shell and shrapnel, mortar bombs
Or whining ricochet?

Who has not felt so worn and tired
He scarce can raise a grin
And mind from body takes control
To will – I won't give in!

Who has not spent cold sleepless nights
On guard against surprise?
Or left his pal to breathe his last,
And on, with bitter eyes?

Who has not heard the bomber's drone
And felt sweat on his brow?
Who has not lived and walked with death?
Not you – YOU LUCKY COW.

Untitled
Anon

They brought us from Australia to fight the Nazi Huns,
Who're once more on the warpath, well equipped with tanks and guns.
They showed us into Libya, where the guide book says its grand.
But forgets to mention little things like flies and fleas and sand.

Tobruk was chosen for the place for us to strut our stuff.
Old Jerry soon besieged it and began to treat us rough.
He dropped a kindly hint or two as to how we soon would cop it.
Advising us to turn it in, forget the war and hop it.

Now being mad Australian, we just didn't take the drum.
So he sent his diving Stukas and made things darn well hum.
A few blokes took the final count, and some joints got knocked about.
But the damage done as Tommies say, was really "bleeding nowt".

He keeps on raiding with his planes, drops bombs and booby traps.
His soldiers sometime make a move and the lads have frontline scraps.
But months have passed. He must admit it seems we're here to stay
Till the Springboks come to join us, marching up from Bardia way.

And when we're back home again, and all this strife is o'er,
Some silly mug is sure to ask "How did you win the war?"
You can look the bloke right in the face and pat the baby's curls.
Say "We defended old Tobruk where there wasn't any girls".

This Place They Call Tobruk
Sgt JH Cuskelly

There's places that I've been to
I didn't like too well
Now England's far too blooming cold
And Winton's hot as hell.
The Walgett beer is always crook

But each and all are perfect to
This Place They Call Tobruk.

We reckoned "El Agheila"
Was none too flash a place.
El Abeer and Bed Tom too
Weren't in the bloody race.
All the towns this side of Benghazi
We hadn't time to look.
But I'll take my oath they're better than
This Place They Call Tobruk.

I've seen some dust storms back home
That make the housewives work.
Here, there's enough inside our shirts
To smother all of Bourke.
Two diggers cleaned their dugouts
And blankets out they shook
Two colonels perished in the dust in
This Place They Call Tobruk.

The shelling's nice and frequent
And things whistle overhead.
You go into your dugout
And find shrapnel in your bed.
And when the Stukas dive on us
We never pause to look.
We're down our holes like rabbits in
This Place They Call Tobruk.

Rats of Tobruk
(A reply to Lord Haw-Haw's jeers) by a RAT

"Good morning, Rats", the Donkey brayed.
"Rats at the end of your tether.
I hear your nerves are somewhat frayed.
Shall I snap them altogether?
Hee-Haw, Hee-Haw,
I'll snap them altogether."

And he called to his birds of prey,
"Swoop low on the British rats:
They're afraid of the light of day.
They live in caves like bats.
Hee-Haw, Haw-haw,
They live in holes – the Rats."

So the Vultures flocked for the kill,
And they dived on the hospital ships.
And the hospital high on the hill.
They blew the wards to bits.
"Whee – Cr-r-ump,"
They blew sick men to bits.

Then in the Fortress drear,
Which they wouldn't evacuate,
The rats began to stir –
The British are slow to hate.
Rat-a-tat, Rat-a-tat,
The rats sat down to wait.

Full gorged with easy game.
The Vultures flocked once more,
"A hundred plus"' they came,
And dived on the shattered shore.
Eeee-aw, Eeee-aw,
They dived and rose no more.

Crash went the big Ack-Ack,
Ker-plonk went the Bofors guns.
And the little Rats stood back
And spat at the hateful Huns.
Rat-a- tat, Rat-a-tat,
Spat lead at the hated Huns.

The Rats gave a grin to themselves.
And they worked as they always done –
Worked in the dark like Elves,
Unseen by anyone.
The Dock Rats swarmed on the gallant ships
And carried the cargoes away.
Food, ammunition, tanks and guns,
Safe hid by the break of day.

Safe hid and passed to the Desert Rats,
Who guard the outer wire
(And what if we did pinch some of the beer,
A Rat is worth his hire).
And the Desert Rats gnawed at his lines by night.
Creeping up on the Huns like ghosts,
Till he screamed and broke in panic flight,
And we took his hard-pressed posts.

In the grey little country over the sea,
The Bulldog cocked his eye,
"Well done, you Rats of Tobruk," said he
"We hang on you and I."

chapter 10

THE GERMAN EXPERIENCE AND FINAL ASSESSMENT

ROMMEL'S CAMPAIGN

Rommel Papers, pp. 122-6

In the early hours of the 10th April, I drove off in the direction of Tobruk and found 3rd Reconnaissance Battalion 30 miles west of the fortress. Unfortunately, they had not yet started their switch to the right for their outflanking attack. I now ordered General von Prittwitz to launch his attack immediately astride the road to Tobruk and 3rd Reconnaissance Battalion to move up through Acroma to El Adem. I then drove back towards Tobruk again and found the leading troops of the machine-gun battalion in attack ten miles from Tobruk. Heavy British artillery fire from Tobruk soon brought their attack to a halt. We had at that time no real idea of the nature or position of the Tobruk defences. The air shimmered and a sandstorm began to blow up; soon the visibility, which so far had been good, closed right down and I drove back. At midday, Count Schwerin reported to me at a point some 25 miles west of Tobruk that General von Prittwitz had been killed a few hours earlier by a direct hit from an anti-tank gun.

To the 5th Light Division I gave orders, after they were relieved by the Brescia, to thrust forward to the Via Balbia east of Tobruk and close the fortress in. Meanwhile the Ariete had been located at Bir Tengeder and ordered forward to El Adem.

As the situation was rather confused, I spent next day at the front again. It is of utmost importance for a commander to have a good knowledge of the battlefield and his enemy's positions on the ground. It is often not a question of which of the opposing commanders is the higher qualified mentally, or which has the greater experience, but which of them has the better grasp of the battlefield. This is particularly the case when a situation develops, the outcome of which cannot be estimated. Then the commander must go up to see for himself; reports received second-hand rarely give the information he needs for his decisions.

We first jolted in our Mammoth down a freshly made track running south from Acroma, and then turned east to approach the Tobruk-El Adem road about 2½ miles north of El Adem. British tanks and armoured cars were moving about on a ridge in front of us — apparently El Adem had not yet been taken by the 3rd Reconnaissance Battalion. On the high ground north-east of El Adem, we discovered a camp, which the enemy had already abandoned. British artillery was heavily shelling elements of the 5th Light Division standing on the road, and soon the shells began to fall near us. I met Lieut-Col Count Schwerin on the Torbuk-El Adem road and instructed him to close in on Tobruk from the east and prevent any attempts at a break-out. Then I drove back to Acroma to bring up more forces. There was now nothing to be seen of German troops on the south-east front of Tobruk. The roof of the Mammoth made an excellent observation tower and gave us a wide view over the whole country – necessary in that dangerous corner where it would have been only too easy for a British scouting party to have picked us up. At last I found the staff of the 5th Light Division. Soon afterwards 5th Panzer Regiment came up with 20 tanks and the machine-gun battalion; they were immediately sent to attack Tobruk from the south-east. I now went forward again to the assembly area. Scattered British artillery fire was falling at a few points. The attack seemed to be meeting more difficulties in the open desert than I had anticipated.

During the afternoon 3rd Reconnaissance Battalion reported the capture of El Adem and I instructed them to continue the pursuit to Bardia. Other forces were now coming in steadily.

On the 11th April, the envelopment of Tobruk was complete and the first attack began. Stukas attacked the defence works, the layout of which was still completely unknown to us. More troops arrived on the 12th April and it was decided to open up the first major attack on the stronghold that afternoon. Bardia was taken that day by the 3rd Reconnaissance Battalion.

The Brescia Division, which had meanwhile taken over the western front of Tobruk, opened the attack in the afternoon. The 5th Light Division was not too happy about its orders for the attack and raised a number of objections which I had to brush aside. It was a day of driving sand and there was no need to concern ourselves about aimed British artillery fire. The 5th Light Division's attack finally got under way at about 16.30 hours. I drove north in my Mammoth behind the tanks. Enemy artillery scattered shells over the area as the tanks approached, but caused few casualties. The 5th Panzer Regiment halted when they arrived at the break-in point and, of course, came under heavy artillery fire. Finally, the tanks were brought to a standstill in front of an anti-tank ditch, which we were not then in a position to blow in. Tobruk's defences stretched much farther in all directions, west, east and south, than we had imagined. We still had not been able to get hold of any of the plans of the defences which were held by the Italians.

After the failure of this attack, I decided to renew the attempt a few days later when more artillery and the Ariete arrived. In no circumstances was the enemy to be allowed time to complete the organisation of his defence.

For the 13th I ordered a reconnaissance raid by the 5th Light Division in which the reconnaissance groups were, if possible, to penetrate to the crossroad inside the Tobruk defences and blow in the anti-tank ditch. To divert the attention of the enemy command, the Brescia division was to pin down the enemy west of the fortress fire, and, by raising as much dust as possible, to simulate the existence of large-scale assembly.

After the failure of the previous raid on Tobruk, the 5th Light division had lost confidence in itself and was unwarrantedly pessimistic about my plan to open our main attack on the 14th. The division's command had not mastered the art of concentrating its strength at one point, forcing a break-through and rolling-up and securing the flanks on either side, and then penetrating like lightning, before the enemy has had time to react, deep in his rear. My estimate of the enemy at that time was that we had a good chance of executing such an operation with the forces we had. All it wanted was a little initiative and some realistic thinking to find a way. Unfortunately, I had not had the opportunity of training my formations personally before the raid through Cyrenaica, otherwise we would have measured up much better to the tasks which faced us at Tobruk.

There still being no sign of the Ariete, which was to back up the 5th Light Division's attack, I set off myself to bring it up. I met the head of the [Ariete] division 22 miles west of El Adem and ordered its commander, Lieut-Gen [Ettore] Baldassare, to take his force into the area north of El Adem.

At about 18.00 hours, 8th Machine-Gun Battalion began its raid under the excellent leadership of Lieut-Col Ponath. Its objective, as already said, was to demolish the anti-tank ditch and create a bridgehead in the British defence zone. The supporting fire of the German and Italian artillery concentrations was well placed. The 18th AA Battalion's batteries, under the personal command of Major Hecht, brought the enemy strong points under direct fire, obviously with considerable success. The progress of our tanks and anti-tank troops seemed to me to be somewhat on the slow side. The British were scattering the country here and there with artillery fire, but we were suffering no great losses. Evening came and we still had not received no definite reports as to whether the demolition of the anti-tank trench had been successful. It was, however, clear that Ponath had broken into the English positions, formed a bridgehead and thus created the conditions for the next day's attack.

Meanwhile, the position on the Sollum front had become more or less stabilised. Sollum and Cauzzo had been taken and the British were keeping fairly quiet. ....

Start time for the 5th Light Division's attack was now fixed for .0030 hours on the 14th. Artillery Regiment [of Col] Grati and the 18th AA Battalion were instructed to work in closest cooperation with the 5th Light Division. I advise the division to be sure to secure the flanks of its penetration and to bring the artillery up quickly.

The attack opened punctually to time, with heavy artillery support. Ponath soon reported that he was making good progress. At daybreak I drove up to a point about 100 yards south of the wire to see for myself how the operation was developing. The attack seemed to be well under way and light signals were riding in the north. Suddenly British shells began to fall in our neighbourhood and we were forced to withdraw after the aerial of our signals vehicle had been cut through with a splinter. Unfortunately, there was nothing to be seen of the force which should have been covering the flanks, although a penetration had obviously been made through the enemy positions west of the road. I therefore drove straight off to the Ariete and ordered them to follow up.

On returning to Corps HQ at about 09.00 hours, I found a report from the 5th Light Division saying their attack had come to a standstill, caused by the fact that the penetration of the enemy line had been too narrow. Shortly afterwards General Streich and Colonel Olbrich arrived at my HQ. Olbrich reported that he already had his tanks at a point two and a half miles south of the town, but they had come under murderous British fire and had withdrawn to the level of Corps HQ. He added that a large part of the infantry had probably been lost. I was furious, particularly at the way the tanks had left the infantry in the lurch, and ordered them forward again immediately to open up the breach in the enemy line and get the infantry out. I hoped to get the attack moving again after the arrival of the Ariete, and immediately drove back to them to see that they were carrying out my orders. Unfortunately, nothing had been done. I spurred the division on to the utmost speed.

When I returned to the 5th Light Division at about midday, I found that practically nothing had been done because of heavy enemy fire. In these circumstances I had no choice but to abandon the attack on Tobruk for the moment, and try to establish contact with Ponath's battalion and fight a way out for them.

I then drove off to the Ariete for the third time and informed them of my decision. I ordered them to take over the sector south of Ras el Madauer, adjoining the 5th Light Division and accompanied them forward at about 17.00 hours. South-east of Gasr el Glecha they received a few rounds of artillery fire from Tobruk. The confusion was indescribable. The division broke up in complete disorder, turned tail and streamed back in several directions to the south and south-west. Their commander, General Baldassare, was away with me at the time reconnoitring the ground north of Gasr el Glecha; with night coming on, he had the greatest difficulty in getting his division under control again and moving it forward to its allotted position.

We were unable to establish contact with Ponath's battalion on the night 14-15 April. A large part of the battalion had been wiped out. Lieut-Col Ponath himself, who received the Knight's Cross for exploits in Cyrenaica, had been killed.

When the Panzer Army Afrikas eventually broke into Tobruk, on the 20th June of the following year, and took possession of the British positions south of the fork 3 miles south of the town, I found there the remains of several German tanks which had been put out of action by British artillery and anti-tank guns on the 14th April 1941. They had reached the hill and thus gained the most important point of the Tobruk defences. Had the 5th Light Division been in a position to secure its two flanks and thus allow the artillery and the Ariete to follow through the breach, Tobruk would probably have fallen on the 14th or 15th April 1941.

A PANZER OFICER'S NIGHTMARE AROUND TOBRUK

Lt Joachim Schrom, diary in Dan McGuirk, *Rommel's army in Africa,* pp. 77-83

14 April 41

At 0100 hours I am called and ordered to report to the Company Commander. Situation: MG Pioneers have worked a gap through the anti-tank defences; 5 Tank Regt, 8 MG, PAK (A/T), Flak-artillery will cross the gap under cover of darkness and will overwhelm the positions. Stuka attack at 0645 hrs.

0715 hrs. Storming Tobruk. With least possible noise the 2nd Bn, Regt HQ Coy and 1st Bn move off with cars completely blacked out. Bitterly cold. Of course the opponent recognises us by the noise, and as ill luck would have it, a defective spotlight on one of the cars in front goes off.

Soon arty [artillery] fire starts up on us, getting the range. We travel 10km, every nerve on edge. From time to time isolated groups of soldiers appear – the tank support men of 8 MG – and then suddenly we are in the gap. Already the tank is nose first in the first ditch. The motor whines: I catch a glimpse of the stars through the shutter, when for the second time the tank goes down, extricating itself backwards with a dull thud with engines grinding.

We are through and immediately take up file in battle order. In front of us the 8th Coy, then 2nd Bn HQ Coy, then the 5th Coy.

With my troops I travel left of the Coy Commander. With 2nd Bn HQ about 60 men of the 8 MG are marching in sparse groups with Lt-Col Ponath. Tanks and Inf – against all rules. Behind us follow Regt HQ Coy and the 1st Bn, likewise the other arms. Slowly, much too slowly, this column moves forward. We must, of course, regulate our speed by the marching troops. In this way the enemy has time to prepare resistance. In proportion, as the darkness lifts, the enemy strikes harder. Destructive fire starts in front of us now – 1-2-3-10-12-16 and more. 5 batteries of 12cm calibre [25 pounders] rain their hail upon us. The 8 MG Coy presses forward to get at them. Our heavy tanks, it is true, fire for all they are worth, just as we do; but the enemy with his superior force and all the tactical advantages of his own territory makes heavy gaps in our ranks.

Wireless: 0900 hrs ant-tank gun – 1700 metre, tank. We are right in the middle of it with no prospect of getting out. From both flanks armour-piercing shells whizz by at 1000 metres per second.

Wireless: right turn, left turn. Retire. Now we come slap into the 1st Bn which is following us. Some of our tanks are already on fire. The crews call for doctors who alight to help in this Witches' Cauldron. English antitank units are falling upon us with their machine guns firing in our midst; but we have no time. My driver, in the thick of it, says, 'The engines are no longer running properly, brakes not acting, transmission working only with great difficulty.'

We bear off to the right. 600 metres off on the reverse slope, anti-tank guns. 900 metres distant, in the hollow behind is a tank. Behind that in the dip, 1200 metres away another tank. How many? I see only the effect of the fire on the terrace-like dispositions of the enemy. Judging from their width and thickness, there must be at least 12 guns. Above us Italian fighters come into the fray. Two of them crash in our midst. The optical instruments are spoilt with the dust. Nevertheless I register several unmistakable hits. A few anti-tank guns are silenced, some enemy tanks are burning. Just then we are hit, and the wireless smashed to bits. Now our communications are cut off. What is more our ammunition is giving out. I follow the battalion commander. Our attack is fading out. From every side the superior forces of the enemy shoot at us.

'Retire.' There is a crash, just behind us. The engine and the petrol tank are in the rear. The tank must be on fire. I turn around and look through the slit. It is not burning. Our luck is holding.

The poor 8th Machine Gunners! We take a wounded soldier or two on board, and the other tanks do the same. Most of the men have bullet wounds. With its last strength my tank follows others which we lose from time to time in dust clouds. But we have to press on towards the south, as it is the only way through. Good God! Supposing we don't find it? And the engines won't do any more.

Close on our right and left flanks the English tanks shoot in our midst. We are struck in the tracks of the tank, which creak and groan. The lane is in sight. Everything hastens towards it. The English anti-tank guns shoot into the mass. Our own anti-tank positions and 8.8 cm anti-aircraft guns are almost deserted, bur the crews are lying silent beside them. Italian arty which was to have protected our left flank lies equally deserted. English troops run out of their positions, some shooting at us with machine pistols, some with hands raised. With drawn pistols, they are compelled to enter our tanks. The English MGs start up and the prisoners fling themselves to the ground. 1st Lt V Hueslen and my machine gunner lie on the side of my tank which faces the machine gun battalion. We go on, now comes the gap – now the ditch! The driver cannot see a thing for dust, nor I either. We drive by instinct. The tank almost gets stuck in two ditches, blocking the road; but manages to extricate itself with great difficulty. With their last reserves of power, the crew gets out of range and returns to camp. My men remove an armour-piercing high-explosive shell from the right-hand auxiliary petrol tank: 3cm of armour plate bogie cut clean through. The petrol tank shot away. The petrol had run out to this level without igniting! Had it not been for the bogie we should have not got out alive.

At 1200 hours we retire into the wadi to the south. Impedimenta follow. We cover up. Heavy cumulus clouds cover the sky. At intervals from 10–30 minutes, two or three English bombers swoop out of them among the tanks. Every bomber drops four to eight bombs. Explosions all around. It goes on like this until 1900 hrs without a pause. ... [Spotter aircraft, these] hateful birds immediately direct art [artillery] fire over our post. Likewise smoke bombs, which sail down on parachutes, producing a steaming vale.

At 100 hrs, I am invited to accompany Lt Franke-Undheim to the OC, Colonel Olbrich. For the tank battle at Agedabia 2.4.41 Iron Cross 2nd Class. Ordered to the Battalion Commander; the div Officer proposes a short toast. Major Hohmnann says, 'Let us drink first to today. How fortunate that the Regt got out again. How splendidly the men fought – indeed'.

Casualties in the 2nd Bn of the 5 Tank Regt: 10 tanks, a few dead, several wounded, more missing. It went badly for the A-Tank units, the light and heavy AA, but especially with the 8 MGs. The Bn is practically wiped out.

9 AUSTRALIAN DIVISION ASSESSMENT OF THE EASTER BATTLE

G 821/159/1 9 AUST DIV SECRET

17 April '41

NOTES ON THE TACTICS EMPLOYED IN THE ACTION AT TOBRUCH 13/14 APR, 41.

1. Enemy Tactics

Phase 1 During the afternoon 13 Apr AFVs demonstrated over a front of at least 10 miles mainly on the front of 20 Inf Bde due SOUTH OF PILASTRINO and astride the El Adem rd.

Later m/cyclists followed by a staff car approached and appeared to select a HQ in dead ground 4,000 yds from our FDLs.

Next MT appeared and inf began debussing about 4000 yds out. There was little attempt at dispersion and concealment until engaged by our artry and aircraft.

Inf were then brought forward in very small dets to within 1500 yds our FDLs. When within this range MG posts were established and ranged on our forward posts. Fire was opened immediately any movement was seen.

During this phase recce aircraft were used to determine the extent and nature of our defences, particularly along the perimeter where the Tk ditch and wire were obviously being plotted in detail.

Phase 2 After dusk tanks came forward singly and cruised about near the A Tk ditch. Enemy inf then approached and concealed themselves in the A Tk ditch. Sapper parties then disarmed our mines, broke down the sides of the ditch and prepared crossings.

Phase 3 Inf with LMGs and A Tk guns on wheels approached the wire under cover of fire from Hy MGs on our strong posts. Gaps were cut in the wire and men passed through at points midway between strong points. As enemy inf infiltrated they spread out fanwise in rear of our FDLS and held a bridgehead with LMGs an A Tk guns to cover the subsequent advance of tanks and inf.

Phase 4 Before dawn 14 Apr, tanks crossed the ditch, went through the wire and penetrated beyond our strong posts. When behind the line of FDLs the tanks formed up facing their objective (apparently direct line on TOBRUCH) and waited for support tps to come through. Whilst this was being done some tanks and AFVs specially detailed to neutralise our FDLs, circled around the strong posts firing continuously.

As Inf support was not quickly forthcoming the tanks proceeded deep into our position (3 miles) and came up against our A Tk and Arty fire. Many were knocked out and the rest circled about and withdrew through some gaps. The inf attack was unsuccessful.

2. Our tactics The Defence was organised in considerable depth, but very widely dispersed because of the large area to be held. All posts were self contained with all round fields of fire.

   Forward posts endeavoured by fire to prevent recce and preparation of tank gaps. A Tk weapons were sited forward to stop tanks at the ditch, but most guns were sited further back to stop penetration. Reserves were in position ready to counter attack to restore forward localities. Div Inf reserves were further back, together with "I" tanks for counter attack, cruiser tanks, and A Tk guns on wheels.

   The above system proved entirely successful. In the darkness some enemy tanks succeeded in getting inside our wire, but our inf held their ground and engaged the oncoming inf, thus preventing them from exploiting their initial success.

   The location and number of tanks which penetrated was promptly reported to Div HQ. Subsequent movements were carefully plotted and reported, thus making it possible for the Div Reserve of tanks to be placed in a favourable position to intercept. The enemy tanks penetration was finally stopped by A Tank guns and Arty 2 ½ miles SE of Pilastrino where a number of tanks were knocked out, the remainder withdrawing out of the perimeter by the same route. Our tanks, having been placed to intercept this movement engaged the enemy tanks and knocked a number out.

3. Lessons on the above

   Main lessons are:-

   (a) Forward inf must hold their ground, going to cover as tanks pass over, and be ready to engage the oncoming inf with every available weapon
   (b) A Tk weapons of forward posts to engage tanks in front and rear after they pass through.

(c) All weapons to be sited in considerable depth to stop the attack when the impetus is waning, with reserves prepared to counter attack to restore essential localities.

(d) All posts to hold their ground whatever the situation, as by doing enemy success can be localised and dealt with by the tank reserve.

(e) Mines to be laid inside the wire so that they cannot be picked up or disarmed. Where possible small mobile reserve to be held and used for blocking crossings and preventing tanks getting through.

FINALLY, IT IS IMPORTANT THAT UNITS REPORT ENEMY MOVEMENTS IMMEDIATELY AND KEEP HIGHER FORMATIONS FULLY INFORMED SO THAT ACTION CAN BE TAKEN TO PLACE RESERVES IN SUITABLE POSITIONS TO DEAL WITH DEEP PENETRATIONS.

INFORMATION ON NUMBERS AND TYPES OF ENEMY TANKS, THEIR LOCATION AND DIRECTION OF MOVEMENT IS PRINCIPALLY IMPORTANT.

Col (illegible signature)

GS 9 Aust Div

A FINAL ASSESSMENT

Lt-Col Ward A Miller, *The 9th Australian Division versus the German Afrika Korps*, p. 14.

The prime causes for the German failure at Tobruk were piecemealing of forces, a poor assessment of the garrison's defensive strength, and overconfidence. These factors affected the ability of the assault forces to retain the initiative and hold, reinforce and expand their penetration.

In reviewing the Tobruk operations from the point of view of the principles of war, the German attack appeared doomed from the start. In their overconfidence and in their under estimation of the Australians' defensive strength, the Germans failed to adhere to the basic principles of war. Rommel's objective was not attainable. He did not possess the tanks, infantry nor artillery necessary to encircle Tobruk and penetrate to the city while at the same time maintaining his capability to continue a defensive to the Egyptian frontier. His objective had been clearly defined, and he was most decisive about its execution, but when it came to the offensive at Tobruk, he could not retain the initiative nor exploit it. Rommel was unable to mass his forces to concentrate his combat power at the point of penetration. In a manoeuvre to encircle the fortress, he had piecemealed his forces in economy of force efforts, attacking, defending, delaying, and conducting deceptive operations, but failing to allocate enough forces to support the main attack with infantry and a mobile reserve.

Rommel also had serious problems with unity of command, because the 5th Light Division commander strongly objected to his plan. At a critical point, Rommel had taken control from him and then given it back. The Germans also lost the element of surprise, because they could not avoid Australian observation and detection, which interfered with German movements. And finally, the German's plan lacked simplicity, because it called for a night attack against a fortified position without sufficient intelligence or reconnaissance.

Morshead, on the other hand, limited his objective to holding Tobruk at all costs. He was successful because he took the initiative away from the Germans, going on the offensive with a defence based on a program of deep patrolling, air and artillery interdiction, and aerial reconnaissance. Though spread thin in an economy of force effort to cover the 28 mile perimeter, he was able to amass his combat power at a critical time by establishing his defence in depth. This defence included a mobile reserve [2/15 Battalion] placed in position to manoeuvre on short notice to relieve pressure on the defence or, if possible, to take the initiative and exploit a successful defence.

As for unity of command, even though General Lavarack had overall command of the area, General Morshead was responsible for the defence of the garrison. Nonetheless, there was total cooperation between the two, and they shared a common objective.

The Germans never acquired an advantage over the Australians because they were unable to penetrate their security. Again, by the aggressive patrolling air and artillery interdiction, use of snipers, and excellent camouflage, the Australians denied the Germans the opportunity to gain information and kept them continuously off balance.

Furthermore, the Australians achieved surprise at several critical times during the five days of action. For instance, the Germans were thrown completely off guard by the Australians' aggressive use of snipers, bayonets, artillery, and rapid counterattack. The Germans were also surprised when their tanks were ambushed by the 25-pounders and when the Australian infantry allowed German tanks to pass through the initial defences before engaging the dismounted troops that followed. The simplicity of the Australian plan influenced its almost flawless execution. In its implementation, fires were well coordinated, positions were mutually supporting, and counterattack forces were properly rehearsed.

The battle for Tobruk is a set piece for light infantry supported by artillery, armour, and antitank weapons in the defence against a heavier armoured force. At Tobruk, Rommel had been denied a critical objective, and his blitzkrieg tactics had failed. Psychologically, it was a shocking blow to German morale, cohesion, and momentum. For the British and their allies, it provided a long-needed boost in morale.

A captured Panzer officer called Tobruk "a witches cauldron". German prisoners were to refer to it as "the hell of Tobruk", admitting nothing like it had ever happened before. Allied forces had made a lasting impression on the German and Italian forces in North Africa.

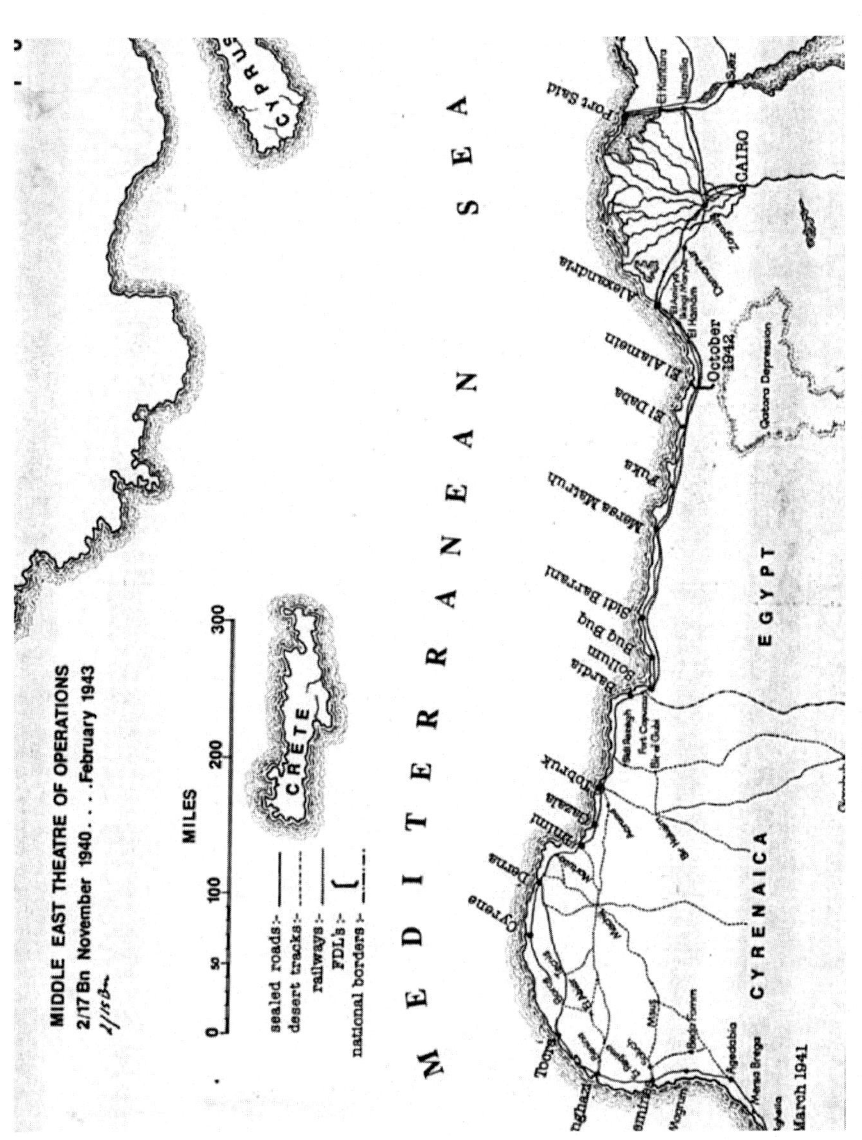

Middle East theatre of operations 1940-43
AG Smith collection

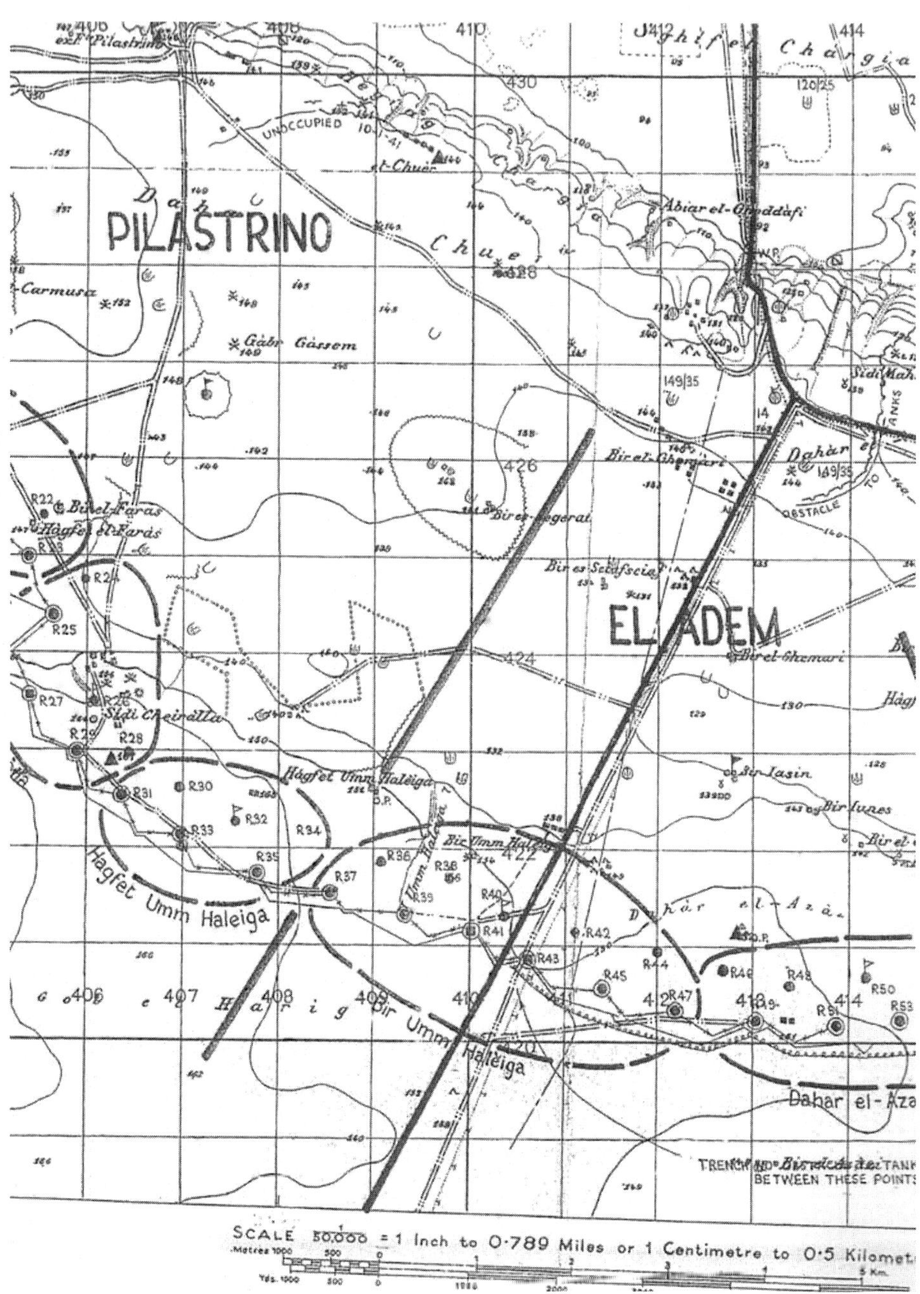

Tobruch Defences 1941
AG Smith collection

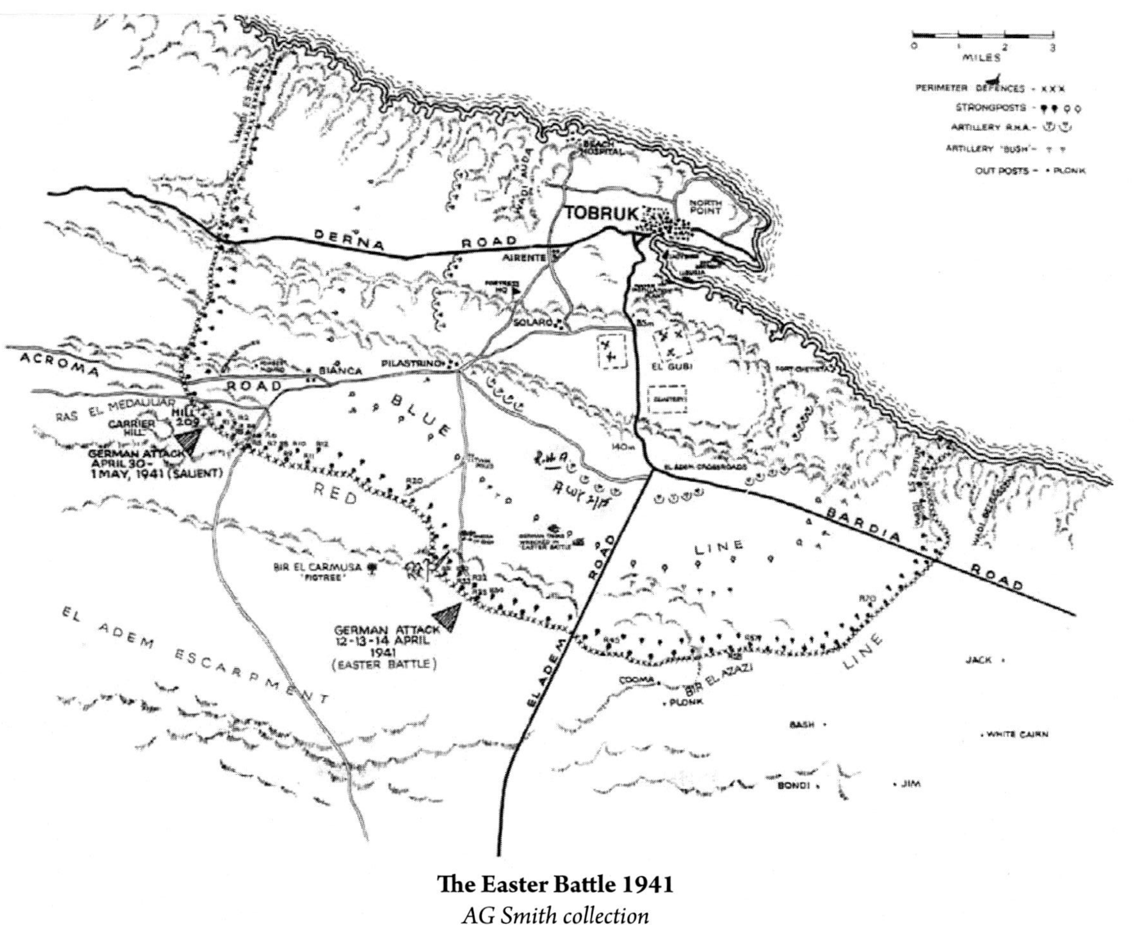

The Easter Battle 1941
AG Smith collection

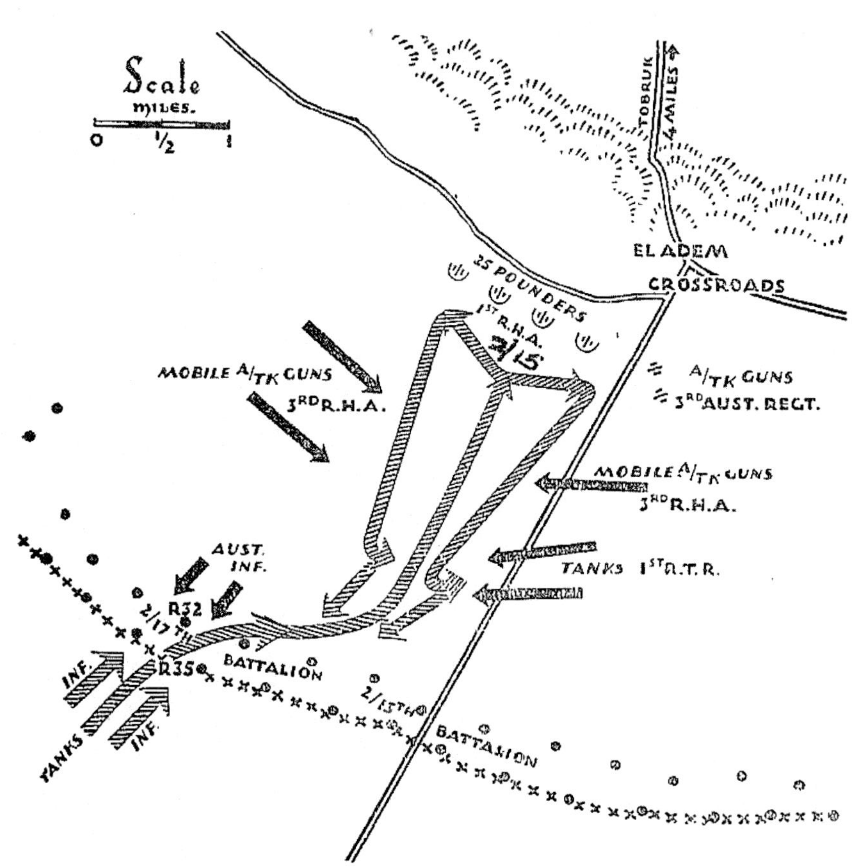

The Easter Battle, 14 April 1941
Chester Wilmot, Tobruk, *1941*

TIMELINE

1940	
13 May	2/15 Bn AIF raised at Redbank Camp and Lt-Col RF Marlan appointed CO.
1 Jul	2/15 Bn sailed from Brisbane on SS Zealandia for garrison duty at Darwin.
27 Oct	2/15 Bn departed Darwin on SS Zealandia and arrived and returned to REDBANK CLUB on 7 Nov 40.
10 Nov	2/15 Bn sent on pre-embarkation leave.
25 Dec	2/15 Bn entrained at REDBANK for SYDNEY.
26 Dec	2/15 Bn embarked on QUEEN MARY in SYDNEY HARBOUR and sailed on 28 Dec with DOMINION MONARCH, AWATEA and ACQUITANIA in convoy.

1941	
12 Jan	Convoy arrived TRINCOMALEE in CEYLON and troops were transhipped to Dutch vessel INDRAPOER.
14 Jan	2/15 Bn arrived at COLOMBO where one days leave was granted before sailing on 16 Jan for MIDDLE EAST arriving in SUEZ on 28 Jan.
29 Jan	Entered SUEZ CANAL and the Bn remained on the ship in the GREAT BITTER LAKE because the SUEZ CANAL had been subject to the laying of magnetic mines by German aircraft.
3 Feb	2/15 Bn disembarked at EL KANTARA and proceeded by train to KILO 89.
4-27 Feb	Training in PALESTINE in preparation for desert warfare.
28 Feb	2/15 Bn commenced move to LIBYAN DESERT.

1 Mar	Arrived at MERSA MATRUH EGYPT, leaving there on 3 Mar and arriving at BUG BUG on that night.
4 Mar	Departed BUG BUG and arrived at TOBRUK, LEAVING there on 6 Mar for DERNA, and moved on to TOCRA.
8 Mar	2/15 Bn left TOCRA, passing through BENGHAZI and arrived at AGEDABIA. That night advance parties left for the front line which was at KILO 789 near MERSA BREGA.
10 Mar	Main body of 2/15 Bn relieved elements of 6th Division and became the most advanced troops in the British lines.
10-21 Mar	2/15 Bn patrolling; improving defences; enemy aircraft strafed our positions and their aircraft more active; reports of German tanks being sighted; reports of German build up in forward area; first Bn casualty when Pte CROKER killed on minefield.
22 Mar	2/15 Bn moved to BARCE.
27 Mar	Our Bn marched nine miles and took up positions at GABEL EL GIRA.
4 April	2/15 Bn moved to Barce
6-9 April	Left Barce at 2100 hours with main body of Battalion moving on coastal road, remainder on inland route. Passed through DERNA and took up a defensive position at AIN EL GAZALA. Part of Battalion including CO and 2/Ic and 154 OR captured by Germans. Left GAZALA during the night 8/9 April and took up position astride TOBRUK- ACROMA road covering withdrawal of 2/13 and 2/17 Bns.
10 April	2/15 Bn moved inside Tobruk defences when siege commenced.

AIF ORGANISATION, ABBREVIATIONS, MEASUREMENTS

AIF ORGANISATION

Brigades of the 2nd Australian Imperial Force consisted of three battalions, formed on a regional basis. The battalions took the titles of their predecessors in World War I, with the prefix 2 preceding the names of the new units (eg 2/15). In addition to the headquarters and support companies, a battalion consisted of four rifle companies, each comprising three 30-man platoons. In the Middle East the strength of a battalion averaged 32 officers to 750 men. An infantry division, made up of 14,000 men, included a headquarters, three brigades, an antitank regiment, a field artillery regiment, engineers and signallers.

ABBREVIATIONS

AA	Anti-Aircraft
AFV	Armoured fighting vehicle
AGH	Australian General Hospital
AIT	Australian Infantry Training (Bn)
AWM	Australian War Memorial
Bde	Brigade
BHQ	Battalion Headquarters
Bn	Battalion
Cap	Captain
CH	*Caveant Hostes* (2/15 Bn AIF Remembrance Club journal)
CO	Commanding Officer (of a battalion)
Col	Colonel
Coy	Company

Cpl	Corporal
CSM	Company Sergeant Major
Div	Division
Gen	General
HQ	Head Quarters
KIA	Killed in action
Lt	Lieutenant
Lt-Col	Lieutenant-Colonel
Lt-Gen	Lieutenant-General
MC	Military Cross
MG	Machine gun
MM	Military Medal
Maj-Gen	Major-General
NAAFI	Navy, Army and Air Force Institute
NCO	Non Commissioned Officer
OC	Officer Commanding (of a company)
POW	Prisoner of War
Pte	Private
RAAF	Royal Australian Air Force
RAE	Royal Australian Engineers
RAF	Royal Air Force
RAN	Royal Australian Navy
Rgt	Regiment
RHA	Royal Horse Artillery
RN	Royal Navy
RSM	Regimental Sergeant Major (of a battalion)
RTR	Royal Tank Regiment
Sgt	Sergeant
VC	Victoria Cross

MEASUREMENTS

1 mile	1.6 kilometres
1 yard	0.914 metre
1 pound (lb)	0.453 kilogram

NOTES

1 Peter Fitzsimons, *Tobruk*. Sydney: Harper Collins, 2006 and 2009.

2 Barton Maughan, *Tobruk and El Alamein*. Sydney: Collins, 1966; Frank Harrison, *Tobruk: The siege reassessed*. London: Brockingham Press, 1996.

3 Robert Lyman, Email to author, 23 July 2009.

4 'Special Order of the Day', issued by Major General Lavarack to the garrison of Tobruk, 14 April 1941. Copied in the field, 15 April 1941. AWM, Canberra.

5 *Kriegstagebuch vom 8 Machinegewehr Bataillon (8 Machine Gun Battalion war journal)*, Essen: 1972.

6 Wolf Heckmann, *Rommel's war in Africa*. New York: Smithmark, 1995, pp. 77-83.

7 Maughan,*Tobruk and El Alemain*, pp.126-9; 154-5.

8 Martin Kitchen, *Rommel's desert war*. Cambridge, Cambridge University Press, p. 79.

9 Gustav Ponath, Award 13 April 1941. List of Knight's Cross of the Iron Cross recipients. Wikipedia.

10 Robert Lyman, *The longest siege Tobruk: The battle that saved North Africa*. Sydney: Macmillan, p. 105.

11 Heckmann, *Rommel's war in Africa*, p. 55.

12 Kitchen, *Rommel's Desert War*. Cambridge: Cambridge University Press, p. 77.

13 Maughan, *Tobruk to El Alamein*, p.9.

14 John Moore, *Morshead*. Sydney: Haldine, 1976, p. 92.

15 Lyman, Email, July 2009.

16 Lyman, *Longest siege*, p. 157.

17 Chester Wilmot, *Tobruk 1941*, Ringwood: Penguin, 1944, p. 116.

18 Maughan, *Tobruk and El Alamein*, pp. 126-9, 154-5.

19 2/15 Battalion war diary, February-April 1941, 8/3/15. AWM52, 2nd Australian Imperial Forces and Commonwealth Military Forces unit war diaries, 1939-45 War, Canberra, AWM.

20 William F Buckingham, *Tobruk: The great siege 1941-42*. Stroud: The History Press, 2009, p. 229.

21 Heckmann, *Rommel's war*, pp. 82-3.

22 Chris Goddard, Email to author, 20 July 2010.

23 Ron Austin, *Let enemies beware: History of the 2/15 Battalion 1940-45*. Rosebud: The 2/15 Battalion, AIF, Remembrance Club, 1995, pp. 60-1.

24 Nazi vehicle-recognition flag captured at Tobruk, REL39783, AWM, Canberra.

25 Wilmot, *Tobruk 1941*, p 93.

26 Res. Line, 10 April 1941, 2/13 Bn Operational Instruction No 1, p.2.

27 Wilmot, *Tobruk 1941*, p. 93; 2/15 Battalion war diary, 11 April 1941.

28 Tobruk garrison, 24 April 1941, 20 Infantry Bde diary, April 1941.

29 2/15 Bn war diary, 20 April p. 88, 21 April p. 89, 20 May, p. 12, 24 May, p. 13, 2 June 1941 p.101.

30 Maughan, *Tobruk and El Alamein*, Map between pp. 212-13; Lyman, *Longest siege*, pp. xviii-xix.

31 Wilmot, *Tobruk 1941*, p. 99.

32 Ibid, p. 101.

33 BH Liddell-Hart ed. *Rommel Papers*, New York: Harcourt, Brace, 1953, p. 126.

34 Maughan, *Tobruk and El Alamein*, p. 154.

35 2/15 Bn war diary, 14 April 1941.

36 Austin, *Let enemies beware*, pp. 1-9.

37 John Neal, Email, 12 October 2010.

38 Austin, *Let enemies beware*, p. 9.

39 Bert Lockie, 'An abbreviated history of the Battalion', *CH*, Souvenir issue, May 1990, p. 6.

40 Don Parker, 'Australian infantry battalion', *CH*, c.1976, pp. 1-2.

41 Alex Connor, 'Approved to wear five service chevrons', *CH*, September 1987, pp. 2 -3.

42 Parker, 'Australian infantry battalion', pp.2-3.

43 George Alford, *CH*, undated p. 3.

44 D Coy war diary, 24 January, p. 18.

45 *Ship's Flashes*, 8 January 1941, p. 1.

46 D Coy war diary, 23 January 1941, p. 17.

47 SF Rowell, 'What of Palestine: Pointers for the AIF', 22 October 1940, insert in D Coy war diary.

48 Connor, *CH*, September 1987, p. 4.

49 D Coy war diary, pp. 31-40.

50 Parker, 'Australian infantry battalion', p. 5.

51 Connor, 'Approved to wear five chevrons', p.4.

52 D Coy war diary, p. 44.

53 Ibid, p. 46.

54 Connor, 'Approved to wear five chevrons,' p. 5.

55 D Coy war diary, p. 49.

56 Parker, 'Australian infantry battalion', p. 7.

57 Connor, 'Approved to wear five chevrons', p.5.

58 Parker, 'Australian infantry battalion,' p. 7.

59 Wilmot, *Tobruk,* p. 71.

60 Buckingham, *Tobruk*, p. 172

61 Lockie, *CH*, May 1990, p. 7.

62 D Coy war diary, p. 51.

63 Parker, 'Australian infantry battalion,' p. 10.

64 Kitchen, *Rommel's desert war*, p. 80.

65 Bert Cowie, 'Glossary', *CH*, p. 406.

66 Connor, 'Approved to wear five chevrons', p.6.

67 John Devine, *The Rats of Tobruk*. Sydney: Angus and Robertson, 1943, pp.33-4, 48.

68 Connor, 'Approved to wear five chevrons', p. 7.

69 Harrison, *Tobruk*, p. 22.

70 Kitchen, *Rommel's desert war*, p.73.

71 Heckmann, *Rommel's war in Africa*, p.38.

72 Lyman, *Longest siege*, pp. 100-1.

73 Jack Anning, interview, 2010.

74 John Moore, *Morshead*. Sydney: Haldane, 1976, pp. 81-3.

75 Liddell-Hart, *Rommel Papers*, p. 132.

76 Heckmann, *Rommel's war in Africa*, p. 41.

77 Liddell-Hart, *Rommel Papers*, p. 118.

78 Buckingham, *Tobruk*, p. 169.

79 Ibid, p. 197.

80 Liddell-Hart, *Rommel Papers*, p. 120.

81 Ibid.

82 Austin, *Let enemies beware*, pp. 48-9.

83 Rosier, Major RC, Diary record of events by QX6260, Bn war diary.

84 Austin, *Let enemies beware*, pp. 178-9.

85 Capt Rolston was the new 2/IC and Lt MacDonald was the new adjutant.

86 D Coy war diary, 9 and 10 April 1941, unpaginated.

87 Timothy Hall, *Tobruk 1941: The desert siege*. North Ryde: Methuen 1984, pp. 45-7.

88 Wilmot, *Tobruk 1941*, pp. 87.

89 Fitzsimons, *Tobruk*, p. 303.

90 Moore, *Morshead*, p. 95.

91 Anthony Heckstall-Smith, *Tobruk: The story of a siege*. London: Corgi, 1959, p. 56.

92 Wilmot, *Tobruk 1941*, p. 91.

93 Moore, *Morshead*, p. 96.

94 Harrison, *Tobruk*, p. 29.

95 See map of Tobruch Defences, January 1941.

96 Moore, *Morshead*, pp. 94-5.

97 Ibid, p. 96.

98 Fitzsimons, *Tobruk*, p. 307.

99 Harrison, *Tobruk*, p. 32.

100 Maughan, *Tobruk and El Alamein*, p. 122.

101 Moore, *Morshead*, p. 96.

102 Ibid, p. 97.

103 Heckmann, *Rommel's war in Africa*, p. 70.

104 Lyman, *Longest siege*, p. 82.

105 Diagrams and map insets to scale of the Easter Monday battle, showing the relationship of the Battalion to 1RHA, appear to place the battalion much closer to the road to Pilastrino and the El Adem road.

106 2/15 Battalion war diary, 10 and 11 April 1941.

107 D Coy war diary, 10-12 April 1941.

108 Ibid.

109 Liddell-Hart, *Rommel papers*, p. 122.

110 Buckingham, *Tobruk*, pp. 207-8.

111 Lyman, *Longest siege*, p. 111.

112 Harrison, *Tobruk*, pp. 41-2.

113 Heinz Schmidt, *With Rommel in the desert*, London: Constable, 1951, p. 39.

114 2/15 Battalion war diary, 11 April 1941.

115 Maughan, *Tobruk and El Alamein*, p. 137.

116 Lyman, *Longest siege*, p. 130.

117 Ibid, pp. 130-1.

118 Kitchen, *Rommel's war in Africa*, p. 85.

119 Buckingham, *Tobruk*, pp. 211-12.

120 Ward A Miller, *9th Australian Division versus the Africa Corps: An infantry division against tanks – Tobruk, Libya, 1941*. Fort Leavenworth: US Army Command and General Staff College, 1986, p. 9.

121 Buckingham, *Tobruk*, p. 218.

122 Maughan, *Tobruk and El Alamein*, p. 141.

123 Maughan, *Tobruk and El Alamein*, pp. 143-4.

124 20th Brigade war diary, 13 April 1941.

125 Buckingham, *Tobruk*, p. 213.

126 Maughan, *Tobruk and El Alamein*, p. 145.

127 Ibid, p. 146.

128 Harrison, *Tobruk*, pp. 49-50.

129 Dan McGuirk, *Rommel's army in Africa*. Sydney: Double Day Book Club, p. 81; 'List of Knight's Cross of the Iron Cross recipients', Wikipedia.

130 Liddell-Hart, *Rommel papers*, p. 124.

131 Harrison, *Tobruk*, pp. 51-3.

132 Kitchen, *Rommel's war in Africa*, p. 86.

133 Maughan, *Tobruk and El Alamein*, p. 148; Heckmann, *Rommel's war in Africa*, p. 77.

134 Ibid.

135 Fitzsimons, *Tobruk*, p.530.

136 Maughan, *Tobruk and El Alamein*, p. 150.

137 Fitzsimons, *Tobruk*, p. 349.

138 Wilmot, T*obruk 1941*, p. 100.

139 HQ 20 Australian Infantry Brigade War Diary, 14 Apriil 1941.

140 Extract from Percival Lyall's testimony on Tobruk.

141 Maughan, *Tobruk and El Alamein*, p. 150.

142 Heckstall-Smith, *Tobruk*, p. 70.

143 Ibid, p. 71.

144 HS Rowan, Diary, 14 April 1941.

145 Jack Anning, interview, August 2013.

146 Ibid.

147 Gordon Wallace, interview, October 2013.

148 Interview, Alfred Greig Smith, 26 September 1987.

149 *Bank Notes*, September 1975, cutting.

150 Interview, Alfred Greig Smith.

151 Ron Yates correspondence, 29 May and 11 June 1941.

152 Harrison, *Tobruk*, p. 54.

153 Wilmot, *Tobruk 1941*, p. 101.

154 K Robinson, *CH*, September 1975, pp. 23-5; Jack anning, interview, August 2013.

155 McGuirk, *Rommel's army in Africa*, p. 80.

156 Ibid.

157 Jack Anning, interview, August 2013.

158 Maughan, Tobruk and El Alamein, p. 152.

159 Ibid.

160 Anning, Wallace, interviews, 2013.

161 Wilmot, p. 101.

162 HQ 20 Australian Infantry Brigade War Diary, 14 April 1941.

163 Maughan, *Tobruk and El Alamein*, p. 153.

164 Gordon Wallace, interview, October 2013.

165 20 Brigade War Diary, 14 April 1941.

166 McGuirk, *Rommel's army in Africa*, p. 80.

167 Percy Lyall interview.

168 Maughan, *Tobruk and El Alamein*, p. 154.

169 2/15thBn AIF War Diary, 14 April 1941.

170 The ditch, a half-dug water channel was 100 yards long, three yards wide and waist high. Interview with Jack Anning, 18 December 2010.

171 Ibid.

172 *CH*, May 1990, p. 22.

173 Bob Scarr interview, September 2010.

174 *CH*, May 1990, p. 22. Wallace, Interview, October 2013.

175 Jack Anning, interview, August 2013.

176 Yates correspondence, 1 6 April 1941.

177 *The Adelaide Advertiser*, 15 March 1947, p. 11

178 AG Smith, Report on patrol, 14 April 1941, 2/15th Battalion War Diary.

179 AG Smith, Report on patrol.

180 Gordon Wallace, Interview, October 2013.

181 Austin, *Let enemies beware,* p. 61.

182 Fitzsimons, T*obruk,* pp. 372-3.

183 Harrison, *Tobruk,* p. 178.

184 TF Cragg, Report on action 13 April 1941, 2/15th Bn war Diary.

185 Lavarack, Special Order of the Day, 14 April 1941, AWM.

186 Ibid.

187 Heckstall-Smith,*Tobruk,* p. 72.

188 David Irving, *Rommel: The trail of the Fox,* London: Wordsworth Military Library, 1999, p.90.

189 Lyman, *Longest siege,* p. 157.

190 Buckingham, pp. 98-100.

191 Miller, *9th Australian Division,* p.12.

192 Wilmot, *Tobruk,* p. 107.

193 *CH,* June 1976, p. 23.

194 Scarr, Interview.

195 Smith, Interview.

196 Miller, *9th Australian Division,* p. 14.

197 Liddell-Hart, *Rommel papers,* p. 124.

198 Wilmot, *Tobruk 1941,* p. xiii.

BIBLIOGRAPHY

OFFICIAL DOCUMENTS

Australian Military Forces, Army Headquarters, formation and unit diaries, 1939-45, 1/5/21, AWM52, DIVISIONS, 9 Australian Division Adjutant General Branch, April 1941, part 1, Canberra: AWM.

2nd Australian Imperial and Commonwealth Military Forces unit war diaries 1939-45 war, 8/2/20, 20 Infantry Brigade, April 1941, Maps, Canberra: AWM.

2/15 Infantry Battalion war diary, February-April 1941 and May-July 1941, 8/3/15. AWM52, 2nd Australian Imperial Force and Commonwealth Military Forces unit war diaries, 1939-45 War, Canberra: AWM.

9 Div War Diary, AWM52, 1/5/20/9, Intelligence log book, March-June 1941, Canberra: AWM.

20th Infantry Brigade War Diary April 1941. 2nd Australian Imperial Forces and Commonwealth Military unit war diaries 1939-45 war, 8/2/20, AWM52, Canberra: AWM.

D Company war diary, 2/15 Infantry Battalion, December 1940-March 1942., 2nd Australian Imperial Force and Commonwealth Forces unit war diaries, 1939-45 War, 8/3/15, AMW52, Canberra: AWM.

Goddard, Chris, Nazi vehicle-recognition flag captured at Tobruk, REL38783, Canberra: AWM, 2011.

GS, 9 Australian Division, 9 Australian Division assessment of the Easter Battle, 14 April 1941, AWM, Canberra.

Kriegstagebuch vom 8 Machinegewehr Bataillon (8th Machine Gun Battalion war journal), Essen: 1972.

Rommel, Erwin, *The Rommel Papers*, ed. BH Liddell-Hart, New York: Da Capo Press, 1953.

Tobruch defences January 1941, map. Overprint by Adv. HQ. WDF, 1941, PUB01050, Canberra: AWM.

ARTICLES/LETTERS/PAMPHLETS

Australian Broadcasting Commission. *The Rats of Tobruk: 242 days of courage*. Audiotape, 1983.

Connor, Alex, 'Approved to wear five service chevrons'. *Caveant Hostes*, September 1987, pp. 1-8.

Condon, Ossie, 'Tobruk battle recalled at manager's farewell'. *Bank News*, September 1972.

Lockie, Bert ed. *Caveant Hostes: The journal of the 2/15 Battalion AIF Remembrance Club*. Souvenir Edition, Brisbane: May 1990.

Ogle, Bob, 'To all who served in an Australian Battalion in World War II'. *Caveant Hostes*, c.1976, pp. A-C.

Parker, Don, 'Infantry Battalion'. *Caveant Hostes*, c.1976, pp. 1-12.

Robinson, Kevin, 'This is Tobruk'. *Caveant Hostes*, September 1975, pp. 23-5.

Rowan, HS, Tobruk diary 1941, private collection.

Rowell, SF, 'What of Palestine? Pointers for the AIF', 22 October 1940, insert in A Coy war diary.

Yates, Ron A, *Letters 1941-42*. CD, Toowoomba: William Yates.

STUDIES

Austin, Ron, *Let enemies beware: History of the 2/15 Battalion 1940-45*. Rosebud: The 2/15 Battalion, AIF, Remembrance Club, and Slouch Hat Publications, 1995.

Buckingham, William F, *Tobruk: The great siege 1941-42*. Stroud: The History Press, 2009.

Cawthorne, Nigel, *Battles of WWII*. London: Arcturus, 2003.

Cochrane, Peter, *Tobruk 1941*. Sydney: Australian Broadcasting Commission, 2005.

Devine, John, *The Rats of Tobruk*. Sydney: Angus and Robertson, 1943.

Fitzsimons, Peter, *Tobruk*. Sydney: Harper Collins, 2007.

Hall, Timothy, *Tobruk 1941: The desert siege*. North Ryde: Methuen, 1984.

Harrison, Frank, *Tobruk: The great siege reassessed*. London: Brockhampton Press, 1996.

Heckmann, Wolf, *Rommel's war in North Africa*. New York, Smithmark, 1976.

Heckstall-Smith, Anthony, *Tobruk: The story of a siege*, London: Corgi, 1961.

Irving, David, *Rommel: The trail of the Fox*, London: Wordsworth Military Library, 1999.

Johnson, Lee ed. *Battles of World War II: Tobruk 1941 – Rommel's first move*. Oxford: Osprey, 2002.

Kitchen, Mark, *Rommel's desert war*, Cambridge: Cambridge University Press, 2009.

Lyman, Robert, *Tobruk: The battle that saved North Africa*. Sydney: Macmillan 2009.

McGuirk, Dan, *Rommel's war in Africa*, Shrewsbury: Airlife, 1993.

Maughan, Barton, *Tobruk and El Alamein*. Canberra: Australian War memorial, 1966.

Miller, Ward A, *The 9th Australian Division versus the Africa Corps*, Kansas: US Army Command and General Staff College, Fort Leavenworth, 1986.

Moore, John, *Morshead*. Sydney: Haldane, 1976.

Schmidt, Heinz Werner, *With Rommel in the desert*. London: George G Harrap, 1951.

Watt, James, *History of the 61st Australian Infantry Battalion: Queensland Cameron Highlanders 1938- 45*. Loftus, NSW: Australian Military History Publications, 2001.

Wilmot, Chester, *Tobruk 1941*. Ringwood: Penguin, 1944.

Young, Desmond, *Rommel*. London: Collins, 1950.

INTERVIEWS/EMAILS

Anning, Jack, 2/15 Battalion veteran, December 2010, August 2013.

Fitzsimons, Peter, author, July 2009.

Goddard, Chris, AWM, July–December 2010.

James, Karl, historian, AWM, February-March 2011.

Lyall, Percy, 2/15 Battalion veteran, September 2010.

Lyman, Robert, author, July 2009.

Neal, John, 2/15 Battalion Remembrance Club, October 2010.

Rowan, Steve, 2/15 Battalion Remembrance Club, August 2010.

Scarr, Bob, 2/15 Battalion veteran, September 2010.

Smith Alan, Lt-Col, March 2011.

Smith, Alfred Greig, 2/15 Battalion veteran, September 1987.

Smith, Raymond, 2/15 Battalion Remembrance Club, October 2010.

Wallace, Gordon, 2/15 Battalion veteran, September 2010, October 2013.

INDEX